AF614045

HIS INCREASE

my decrease for

52 contemplations on worship and the supremacy of God's glory

preston philpott

my decrease for HIS INCREASE:
52 Contemplations On Worship And The Supremacy of God's Glory

published by His Increase Ministries

International Standard Book Number 978-0-6151-8341-1

Cover Image by Chris Huff
Used by permission from www.designsbychris.com

Cover Design by preston philpott

Printed in the United States of America

For information:
His Increase Ministries, in care of Corner-Stone Baptist Church
6933 Highway 11 • Jefferson, GA • 30549

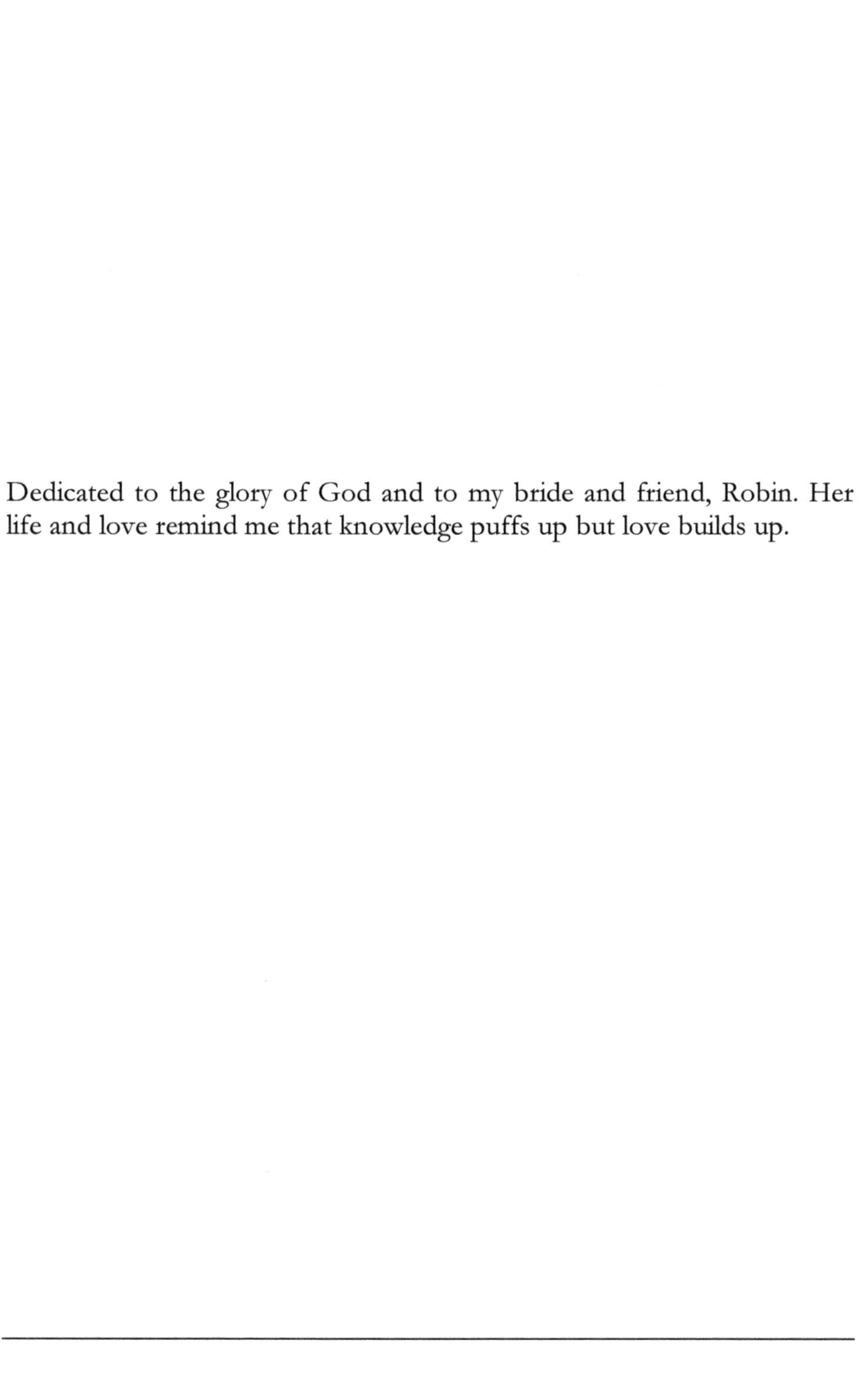

Dedicated to the glory of God and to my bride and friend, Robin. Her life and love remind me that knowledge puffs up but love builds up.

Contents

Introduction

In March of 2006 Robin and I moved from Corinth, TX to help start a new church in Northeast Georgia called Corner-Stone Baptist Church. These short essays were written between the months of April 2006 and June 2007 in hopes that they would help inform and enrich the worship that our new church would give to God.

While these entries were written for mature believers, I think the un-churched would welcome the candor. To hear that humanity's role in the universe is so shockingly tiny in comparison to God's glory may be exactly what they need to hear! In fact, according to the Word of God that is exactly what we all need to know. In any case, I have always welcomed feedback … preston@corner-stone.org.

There are 52 total, one for each Saturday of the year to prepare our hearts for the following Sunday morning worship service. They are numbered in the order they were written. I had thought to group them by content but I noticed, among other things, an acceleration or lift-off in their original sequence. Not wanting to remove whatever small amount of continuity there was, I left them.

Initially I called them ditties, then igniters, now essays or entries or whatever. Call them what you like. My earnest desire is that they challenge your heart and mind and move them toward a greater appreciation of God's glory and love.

The title in no way was meant to imply similarity in content or substantive quality with Oswald Chamber's classic. It is simply the most fitting way I could express what I wanted to say with these entries and with my life.

My sincerest appreciation goes to family and friends who have contributed to the content and clarity of these essays through questions and suggestions. Special thanks to my mother, Kathy Philpott, and my grandmother, June Wolfe, for helping me prepare these for publication.

Preston Philpott
Jefferson, GA
December 2007

One

MAY GOD BE OUR PREFERENCE

Without a sensitivity to the Spirit, we can reduce worship to an experience that fits comfortably within the parameters of our own preferences . . . This is understandable, but it sets the risky precedent of reducing worship – and our concept of God – to what makes us comfortable.

Steve Fry, Rekindled Flame

And above all you must be asking which door is the true one; not which pleases you best by its paint and paneling. In plain language, the question should never be: 'Do I like that kind of service?' but 'Are these doctrines true: Is holiness here? Does my conscience move me toward this? Is my reluctance to knock on this door pride, or my mere taste, or my personal dislike of this particular door-keeper?'

C.S. Lewis, Mere Christianity

ONE OF THE MOST INTRIGUING AND FASCINATING THINGS about the Body of Christ is the diversity of its members. The late Keith Green wrote a beautiful song celebrating our diversity called "Stained Glass." But the different and unique aspects that are able to create a stunning mosaic of our lives can also be the things that drive so many believers apart.

When our personal tastes and preferences determine the expressions of worship in which we will or will not participate, we need a shift in our perspective. To put it more bluntly, if the expressions of worship are biblical imperatives or otherwise scripturally encouraged, it does not really matter what we like or dislike because the worship is not for us – it belongs to God!

We are the worshipers, not the worshiped. Therefore, in regard to worship services our personal tastes acquiesce to the more relevant objective of setting our mind's attentions and our heart's affections on God alone.

It is not a matter of right or wrong that we all feel more comfortable in certain settings or that we may find it easier to engage in worship when we find ourselves in those settings. Furthermore, God does not require that we pretend that we do not have personal tastes and preferences; only that those personal tastes and preferences do not determine our participation in worship.

There is a divine liberation when we put our comforts at the feet of Jesus and simply ascribe worth to the One we love. And in the light of His glory these forfeitures or "sacrifices" of our personal tastes and preferences that would keep us from our intended purpose (His magnification) are always exposed for what they are – enemies of His glory. May God be our preference.

Two

WORSHIP STARTS WITH SEEING GOD

People fashion their God after their own understanding. They make their God first and worship him afterwards.

Oscar Wilde, Irish Poet, Novelist, Dramatist, Critic 1854-1900

WE SEE GOD MOST CLEARLY IN THE PERSON OF HIS SON, JESUS. It was Jesus himself who said, "*He who has seen me has seen the Father*" (John 14:9). Jesus was not speaking only literally here. For every believer since His ascension has felt His truth and has spiritually seen His glory by the power of the Holy Spirit as He testifies to the truth of the message now handed down to us in scripture.

It seems the Apostle Peter encountered some of the same cute anti-Christian philosophy that Wilde offered his generation. And he answered it by saying, "We did not follow cleverly invented stories when we told you about the power and coming of our Lord Jesus Christ, but we were *eyewitnesses* of his majesty."

Every testimony of scripture that describes a human encounter with God, contains a confession of prior ignorance. Perhaps Job said it better than anyone when he said, *"My ears had heard of You, but now my eyes have seen You!"* (Job 42:5)

No true worship experience will ever happen without actually *seeing* in our humbled hearts, the one true living God. The beautiful news is that God wants us to see Him so that we may treasure Him!

Wilde was wrong about the God of the Bible. The kind of thinking expressed here by Wilde discloses the feeble understanding of one never having seen the God who has revealed Himself in scripture, in the person of His Son Jesus and through the person of His Holy Spirit.

For within the pages of God's Word we find a God who is unimaginable; in His ominous numinous power, in His grace, in His mercy, in His love and in His unending, white-hot, relentless pursuit of us. No person could have ever imagined Him. He is too inscrutably glorious. Indeed, we could never have imagined Him, but He has graciously revealed Himself to us.

Three

IT IS UNNATURAL NOT TO PRAISE GOD

"I tell you, if these become silent, the stones will cry out!"

Luke 19:40

THE MILLENNIA LONG ANNUAL REMEMBRANCE of the most terrifying event of the Old Testament is the setting of Christ's triumphal entry. It is the *Feast of Unleavened Bread* or *Passover*. Hundreds of thousands if not millions have descended upon Jerusalem and Jesus is the hottest topic of conversation.

The excitement over the hope that Jesus may be the One who will liberate Israel and establish a Kingdom with no end has inebriated the masses. And the whispers have churned into shouts of "Hosanna!" between the years since Jesus was baptized and the situation to which we now look.

All of creation, the entire history of the made universe has been hurtling toward this very moment in time and nothing could keep a chorus of praise from rising up and recognizing the God of it all. It is as if all the works of God, every word He had spoken, all the life that He had breathed out were now beginning to return to Him in praise!

But be on guard, for the enemies of God loathe His magnification. And where God is truly being worshiped there will be ungodly resistance. You can count on it. There are many who do not want His praise to be voiced or heard? (2 Samuel 6, Matthew 2, Mark 14, John 12, Mark 10, and here in Luke 19)

But here the praise that was and is and will always be rightfully God's was now tearing its way through the very fabric of the physical reality, which He created! What Jesus says is not mere hyperbole. It is the God of everything, the One who can make dry bones dance, part the red sea, walk on water and raise Himself back to life saying, *"I will be praised!"*

I believe Christ uses this peculiar image of stones crying out to reveal something supremely important regarding the intended purpose of man.

What, after all, would be more unnatural than lifeless stones become living choirs to the King of Majesty? Only the unthinkable act of those created, designed and redeemed for this purpose keeping their quiet! It is our great privilege to carry on, until He returns –and then forever, the praise begun at "*the fullness of time.*" Blessed is He who comes in the name of the Lord!

Four

EASTER IS THE FULCRUM OF OUR WORSHIP

The joyful news that He is risen does not change the contemporary world. Still before us lie work, discipline, sacrifice. But the fact of Easter gives us the spiritual power to do the work, accept the discipline, and make the sacrifice.

Henry Knox Sherrill

WHEN SHERRILL SAYS THAT THE "FACT" OF EASTER GIVES us spiritual power he must mean that the atoning crucifixion of our perfect Lord, His then resurrection, and His subsequent ascension was the divine formula that empowers us to live the life. And just as importantly, it enables our wandering hearts to worship God in the only manner He may be worshiped.

The resurrection and ascension of our Lord was the guarantee that our worship could finally be what He said it would be – *"in spirit and truth."* (John 4:23) For it is the Holy Spirit who is our Enabler:

"For if I do not go away, the Helper will not come to you … He will guide you into all truth." (John 16:7, 13).

And, *"He will bring glory to me (Jesus) by taking from what is mine and making it known to you. All that belongs to the Father is mine. That is why I said that the Spirit will take from what is mine and make it known to you."* (John 16:7-15 NIV, parenthesis mine)

Two of the great evidences of Jesus' resurrection are the inexorable belief of His followers in its fact and the boldness in which they proclaim it. Compare the feebleness of the disciples prior to Christ's ascension and their resulting audacious and gritty determination to proclaim the risen Lord following Pentecost.

What I'm getting at and what I believe is that the fact of Easter is the fulcrum upon which our worship pivots.

If Easter is any thing other than what the Bible purports it to be – a genuine historical fact – we may assume that all believers in its counterfeit truth have basically been carried along by some kind of erroneous (albeit unexplainable and undying) euphoria. And our worship is no more God-truthed or Spirit-infused than any other human activity.

But if the fact of Easter and all that it represents to genuine followers of Christ is true, then we can rest in the knowledge and certainty that our worship is acceptable and pleasing to God because God is at its origin! Thank you Jesus!

Five

WORSHIP IS A GIFTED RESPONSE

Worship is our response to the overtures of love from the heart of the Father.
Richard Foster

IN ONE OF OUR PREVIOUS ENTRIES (2) we spoke about worship being the result of seeing God. We understand, of course, that God always initiates the seeing part. In other words, we look to see only because God, in His grace, wants us to see; He wants to reveal something about Himself. Or perhaps more precisely, He desires simply to reveal Himself.

The difference amounts to something like reading that God forgives sins versus having your sins forgiven. Or reading that God loves and cares for His children versus being adopted and having God lavish His love and affection on you.

In light of these things Richard Foster may have noticed the best one word equivalent to the word worship that we have – response. *"Worship is our response…"*

In fact, I propose that most people today may understand a church sign that read *"Responding to God at 9:30 or 11:00"* better than they would a sign that read *"Worship at 9:30 or 11:00."*

But let us be clear that while worship necessarily means we are responding, just because we are responding does not necessarily mean that we are worshipping. For terms such as "traditional worship" or "contemporary worship" are misnomers – there are no such things. There is only worship or no-worship. However, we could and do have "traditional responses" and "contemporary responses." But that is another entry.

The point remains that it is often helpful to evaluate how our worship is going by examining it in the light of a response. Spiritual and physical behavior as it relates to corporate worship is a great place to start. You may want to begin by asking some diagnostic questions. How have I been responding? How should I be responding according to God's Word and all that He has shown me? How will I respond? And there are many more.

It may help to ask ourselves how we might respond if royalty from another country were to enter our home, or if we were to enter theirs. Would we be largely indifferent? What if that person had done something remarkably costly for us? Perhaps the best question to find the answer to is, "What would God say about our response?"

Let us pray that we are the worshipers that God seeks, responding to Him in spirit and truth.

Six

THE BEAUTIFUL DESIGN OF WORSHIP

Worship is to quicken the conscience by the holiness of God, to feed the mind with the truth of God, to purge the imagination by the beauty of God, to devote the will to the purpose of God.

William Temple, 1881-1944 Archbishop of Canterbury

WILLIAM TEMPLE PENNED ONE OF THE MOST CONCISE and informed definitions of worship I have ever read. And within Temple's definition we find perceptively described God's beautifully simplistic and systematic arrangement of communing with Him.

God, as we have decided, is always the initiator. Temple describes it as a quickening or a "coming alive" of the conscience. It is the result of God revealing the huge difference between His holiness and our sinfulness.

This recognition is also (and not incidentally) the first truth with which we feed our minds. The truth of God's absolute uprightness and the truth of our depravity are the main ingredients to the perfect mind-food. They are, combined, the great "truth" in the crowning statement on worship by Christ Himself in John 4 that we would worship in spirit and truth.

The feeding of our minds with matters of truth necessarily leads us to the beauty in God's merciful dealing with sinful humanity. What would be the shame of the world (crucifixion) would be the most unimaginable beauty and incomprehensible glory of God! And it is within His beauty that we find our imaginations' most powerful cathartic.

And so, following God's perfect design, worship brings us to the point of obedience. No one has ever had a worship experience whose will was not subsequently irresistibly bound to God's. In fact, we could say that the worship experience is "irreducibly complex" to borrow a term from our Intelligent Design friends. It is all or nothing.

The person who defies or ignores the will of God but says that he or she is a worshipper of God are either lying or ignorant. For worship includes obedience, it is not an option; it is part of the beautiful and irreducible design. (This thought will be the main point of emphasis in next weeks' entry.) Jesus said it plainly, *"If you love me, you will obey."* John 14:15 see also John 14:21, 23, 24.

Seven

WORSHIP IS IRREDUCIBLY COMPLEX

I am a committed Christian. I worship in my own way. That's my business. That's not the business of the Pharisees who are going to preach to me about what I do and then do something else.

Contemporary Politician and former Presidential candidate

IF WE HAVE NOT BEEN STRAIGHT TO THE POINT in our previous entries let us be so now – we do not get to worship in our own way – we worship God's way or we do not worship Him at all. For worship, to be sure, is completely God's business.

And God has determined that worship is a full-orbed task, an "irreducibly complex" system if you will. Irreducible complexity is a term coined by Michael Behe, PHD, Lehigh University Professor of Biochemistry and Molecular Biology in his best selling book Darwin's Black Box. Behe is at the forefront of the Intelligent Design movement and one of the biggest thorns in the side of Darwinian Evolutionists. Behe explains irreducible complexity to investigative journalist Lee Strobel like this:

"You see, a system or device is irreducibly complex if it has a number of different components that all work together to accomplish the task of the system, and if you were to remove one of the components, the system would no longer function … the system has to be fully present in order for it to function."

Anytime someone says something like, "*I worship in my own way,*" it discloses something deeper. We can be sure that with this belief comes worship with one of its components missing. It is pride that resists the fact of worship's all or nothingness. It is an erroneous notion that we have the privilege to agree with God's Word in some areas and marginalize what we do not like so much. As if to say that so long as we are sincere we are allowed to worship in our own way.

Not the least of many problems with this line of thinking is that despite our sincerest intentions we cannot trust ourselves to worship in the right way! Jeremiah 17:9 reveals that our hearts are "*deceitful above all things, and desperately evil.*" Proverbs 14:12 tells us that "*there is a way that seems right to a man, but in the end it leads to death.*"

So we see that while it may be true that our worship is not really the business of other people (Pharisee or not) – let us be advised that our worship is under the scrutiny of God! It is the committed Christian that says, *"I worship God's way."* This is why searching the scriptures for God's description of true worship would be difficult to over-emphasize.

Eight

RESPONDING TO HIS MERCIES

. . . by the mercies of God, present your bodies a living and holy sacrifice . . .
Romans 12:1

THE ONLY REASONABLE RESPONSE TO THE WORK OF GOD in Christ according to scripture is described as a peculiar divine oxymoron – "a living sacrifice." Modern vernacular would have us say something like "living dead" or "dead-man walking."

Zombies have never really captivated my attention. But I have thought long enough about them at one time to determine what makes them effectively scary. How could something so slow (albeit persistent) be so frightening? Besides their stereotypical hideousness the answer is simple – they have nothing to lose.

Suppose we as Christians really worshiped as if we had nothing to lose. Would our worship look any different? Do concerns over losing something keep us from effectively worshiping? Do fears of embarrassment (losing self-security), rejection (losing self-worth), humiliation (losing self-respect), etc. sometime determine the lengths to which we are willing to go to ascribe worth to God?

Paul says that by God's mercies, or in view of God's goodness, live as if you had nothing to lose! While it is true that we do forfeit certain things in our commitment to follow Jesus, in the light of God's goodness towards us we can be sure that whatever we give up we gain immeasurably more. Philippians 3:8 categorizes our losses as rubbish/refuse. It is the equivalent of getting something extremely valuable in exchange for ashes.

All of this is fairly elementary I know. But the fleshing out of our worship under the charge of total abandonment is not. So after reading Paul's admonition we should be asking ourselves a question:

"If the natural result of seeing God's mercies, His greatness, His goodness is a life in worship that is fearless and relentless how is my worship measuring-up?"

If our answer to this question is that our worship looks very little like it should, may we then beseech God to help us see His mercies more clearly. These views of God are our impetus and our only enduring impulsion to live lives as if we had nothing left to lose!

Nine

MUSIC IN WORSHIP

When you use music to worship you are not attempting to entertain.
Cliff Richards, ex-rock musician

WHILE THERE MAY BE AN ELEMENT OF ENTERTAINMENT in worship as it relates to our entertaining God as we sing to Him, that God is our audience, I do not believe any deep and plenary theology of worship can be formed around this idea. So Richard's quote provides a good springboard for further thought.

Some worship leaders are under the false impression that it is their role to engender worship. As if worshippers are gathered to respond to the music and songs. But that is theological quicksand. For God is the only "Prompter" and we simply use music as one way to respond to His prompting.

Over-emphasizing the importance of music will only reveal that music is woefully unable to sustain the role of Prompter, which solely belongs to God.

The closer someone is to believing that music is in some way worship itself, the closer that individual is to being disappointed in music's inevitable failure to live up to that distorted idea. Viewing music simply as a tool or medium in which to worship God actually enriches the use of it.

And still music is special. Music, we can biblically prove, has been around, if not for all eternity in the heart of God, at least since some of the 'firsts' of God's creation. We can be sure that God loves music for He is a musical being! So what is it about music that is so effectual in helping us worship God?

Bound with the fact that God made us musical is the truth that our emotions are easily carried along by melodies and harmonies and rhythms and poetry. So music empowers us to express to God what we cannot express with words alone! It is in one sense God's gift to us and our gift right back to Him.

And while it may be wise to guard against emotionalism in our worship, equal care should be taken to ensure that we bring our emotions to glorify God. Our emotions after all are included in the irreducibly complex system of our very make-up – our hearts, souls, minds and strength.

If we have been guilty of believing music is for our entertainment, we have actually over-valued it and under-utilized it in the same instant. Let us begin to use music for what it is really worth for it is only then we can use it for all it is worth!

Ten

ARE WE PREPARING TO WORSHIP

Enter His gates with thanksgiving and His courts with praise...

Psalm 100:4

A woman came to him with an alabaster jar of very expensive perfume...

Matthew 26:7

MOST BIBLICAL SCHOLARS BELIEVE THAT THE WOMAN in Matthew 26 had somewhere in the realm of a Roman pound's worth of perfume. The Roman pound was roughly the equivalent of 12 ounces, so that the alabaster jar and its content would have been worth more than a years wages.

Although there is some historical evidence that Hebrew women carried small vials of perfume on chains around there necks, it would seem unlikely that any woman regularly carried one with this volume and value. On the contrary, it would have been something left at home in a secure place. But this was a special occasion. She was preparing to worship.

I do not believe that the "very expensive perfume" impressed Jesus so much as her premeditated and determined expression of love. Christ's response to this woman's worship should cause us to carefully examine all aspects of this woman's posture. It began with preparedness.

There is ordinarily something intrinsically more valuable and estimable in an intentional gift. If I have come once before His throne empty handed because I failed to give our togetherness proper forethought I have done so too often.

Filling our sanctuaries with expensive things is not the answer. But in keeping with this woman's worshipful example we should be bringing costly gifts. And I do not know anyone who gives a costly gift without any forethought. Expensive gifts perhaps, but not costly ones. The alabaster jar of perfume was expensive, but the giving of it (the gifting) was costly.

The woman's gift, among other things, would have represented her past, present and future. I do not have the space to unpack all of what I mean by that here (read #51 for some unpacking) but the point should not be lost – she had prepared to give something that was significantly costly.

In the very least, this woman brought all the attentions of her mind, all the affections of her heart, and all of the intentions of her will. And she was prepared to give them all beforehand. If worship is to begin upon our entering (Psalm 100:4), it means anticipatory hearts outside His gates!

Eleven

GUARDING OUR STEPS IN WORSHIP

Guard your steps as you go to the house of God and draw near to listen rather than to offer the sacrifice of fools...

Ecclesiastes 5:1

WE ARE PRESENTED WITH TWO OPTIONS AS WE DRAW NEAR to God: we can be thoughtful in our listening or we can *offer the sacrifice of fools.*

Listening should not and does not preclude singing and praying if they are *informed.* That is, if they are informed by our listening. In fact, they should be evidences of our listening!

Rather, let the person guard their steps who engages in nothing more than what Alistar Begg calls "spiritual doodling" and believes it a good enough response to the living God. There are two primary characteristics that define the fool – (1) rebellion (Psalm 107:17) and (2) presumption – thought or action without an informed context (Proverbs 13:6).

Remember the disciples' posture after Jesus had calmed the tempest? Mark 4:41 tells us that they were terrified. Their fear shifted from the squall that threatened their tiny lives to the One who held the entire universe in His hands. Their mortification stemmed from the realization that all of their pettiness, indecencies and trifling were shamelessly on display before the Omni-One all the while.

Job had a similar experience. Job initially believed that he would have plenty to say the next time that he and God had some one on one time (read Job 23:1-7). But it is an understatement to say that his encounter with God helped to inform and clarify what he presumed to know (read Job 42:1-6).

I would not disagree with the person who says that we might be better off with a little less singing and praying and a little more listening and waiting. (Probably the two most challenging exercises for the Christian.) But I do not believe that that is the crux of Ecclesiastes 5:1. I believe our text is more concerned with our limited perspective. Verse 2 informs verse 1 – *"For God is in heaven and (we) are on earth ..."*

That is the real matter about guarding our steps. God is God and we are not. Our familiarity and flippancy will not do! Let us remove from our worship any spiritual white noise, which is the *sacrifice of fools.* Everything we do and say is utterly dependent on His mercy and grace. There needs to be a permanent watermark affixed to all that we offer that perceives our total dependency to His all-sufficiency!

Twelve

WORSHIP AND THE WORD OF GOD

They (all the people) asked Ezra the scribe to bring the book of the Law of Moses ... [5]and when he (Ezra) opened it, all the people stood up... [6]Then Ezra blessed the Lord the great God. And all the people answered, "Amen, Amen!" while lifting up their hands. Then they bowed low and worshiped the Lord with their faces to the ground.

Nehemiah 8:1,5,6

FIFTY PLUS YEARS WITHOUT IT, would give anyone plenty of time to gain a proper perspective on God's written word. This remnant was not looking to be entertained; they did not ask Ezra to bring out the drama bears. They were hungry for scripture. I wonder if there remains the spirit of that remnant today? In regard to the written word of God – they stood in honor of it; they worshiped God for it; they wept over the content of it and rejoiced in their comprehension of it.

It is difficult to determine exactly why the people wept over what they heard because it is clear from verse 12 that they did not initially fully understand what they were hearing. In any case, they understood enough about God to believe that His word required a response; it is not something that should be received with indifference! Indeed, His Word accomplishes that which it was, is and will be sent out to do (Isaiah 55:11).

Books could be written on the ecclesiological material in this short chapter, from the first pulpit (verse 4) to the responsibility of church staff to *teach* the Word of God (verses 8, 9, 11, 12), to the heart of God's people for His word (verses 3, 6). But how does this passage inform our worship today?

There is the danger of interpreting this passage to mean that God's written word is to be the center of worship. It is not. The bible is not God. But without God's written word we have no other objective way of knowing whom we worship, why we worship Him and how He should be worshiped. The bible is God's primary chosen way of revealing Himself to us. All other ways of revealing are plumbed and measured against His written testaments.

Worship should most often be enthralling and may even be entertaining. But we must shake ourselves from the spiritually dwarfing fallacy that worship **is to be** entertaining. May God grant us the remnant heart that cannot take the scriptures too seriously, nor teach them too scrupulously, nor listen to them too conscientiously - for these purify, refine and ignite our worship!

Thirteen

WHO'S ASKING THE QUESTIONS?

Let's face it; God has a big ego problem. Why do we always have to worship him?

Modern American Comedian, Actor, Writer, Producer

DO YOU NOT KNOW? HAVE YOU NOT HEARD? I am the everlasting God, the Creator of the ends of the earth. I will not grow tired or weary, and my understanding no one can fathom. I am the Alpha and the Omega, who is and who was and who is to come.

To whom will you compare me? Or who is my equal? Lift your eyes and look to the heavens: Who created all these? I brought out the starry host one by one, and call them each by name. Because of my great power and mighty strength, not one of them is missing.

Who has measured the waters in the hollow of their hand, and marked off the heavens by the span, and calculated the dust of the earth by the measure, and weighed the mountains in a balance, and the hills in a pair of scales? Who has directed my Spirit or as my counselor informed me? With whom did I consult and who gave me understanding?

And who taught me in the path of justice and taught me knowledge? And informed me of the way of understanding? Have you ever in your life commanded the morning, and caused the dawn to know its place? Do you send the lightning bolts on their way? Do they report to you, 'Here we are'?

Who has a claim against me that I must pay? Everything under heaven belongs to me. I am not a man, that I should lie, nor a son of man, that I should change my mind. Do I speak and then not act? Do I promise and not fulfill?

What is your life? You are a mist that appears for a little while and then vanishes. All men are like grass, and all their glory is like the flowers of the field. But I demonstrated my own love for you in this: While you were still sinners, I died for you.

I created your inmost being; I knit you together in your mother's womb. My thoughts of you outnumber the grains of sand. And I am a forgiving God, gracious and compassionate, slow to anger and abounding in love. For from me and through me and to me are all things. And as I live … every knee shall bow to me, and every tongue shall give praise to God! So then each of you will give an account of yourself to me.

(Isaiah 40:28; Revelation 1:8; Isaiah 40:25, 26, 12, 13, 14; Job 38:12, 35; Job 41:11; Numbers 23:19; James 4:14; Isaiah 40:6; Psalm 139:13, 18; Nehemiah 9:17; Romans 11:36, 14:11-12)

Fourteen

THE GLORY OF GOD

And he [Moses] said, 'Please show me your glory!' ... But He [God] said, 'You cannot see My face; for no man shall see Me, and live.

Exodus 33:18, 20

I SUSPECT THAT OUR FAMILIARITY WITH THE WORD *GLORY* has kept us from paying proper attention to its substantive content within scripture. Or perhaps the word has been so overused that we have replaced its richness with some kind of ambiguous religious nostalgia. To whatever degree these statements are true I feel we must improve.

Glory may be the one word in all of scripture that we must not 'under'-understand. For the most important thing to God is His own glory! John Piper said it well that God's glory is "the invincible end for which he created the world." If this is true we must not settle for an 'under' informed understanding of God's glory.

God's glory begins with His divinity (another word in desperate need of an over-haul), His awesome, absolute supremacy and perfect mode of being. Thus, Moses was asking to see God's otherness. And God answers, *"You cannot see my face."* This is God's way of saying two mind-blowing things at once.

Firstly, He is saying, *"You are not able to see all of who I really am, period."* 1 Timothy 6:16 teaches us that no one has seen or can (is able) see God. Secondly, God is saying, *"You can not handle the truth!"* In other words, if Moses was able to see God's "face," that being the essence of His eternal perfect-ness, he would implode!

Ontologically (the true stuff/essence of), God does not have natural form (face, arms, legs, etc.) for He is a spirit. The use of anthropomorphisms (naturalistic human traits/characteristics) is God's way of helping us understand His total uniqueness. So the use of "my face," is important. Ask yourself why?

Also, although it is something of a side note to the direction of this particular entry, may we never forget the beautiful, reassuring words of Christ, *"Anyone who has seen me has seen the Father"* (John 14:9).

So what does all this mean for us? What does it then mean to say that the reason for our existence is to bring God glory? It is not as if we can add anything to eternal perfect-ness! True, and yet it is God's unimaginable condescension to permit us to participate! And so, if ever we are declaring and proclaiming God's glory we are at once bringing Him glory.

Fifteen

THE CENTRALITY OF GOD IN WORSHIP

As long as you notice, and have to count, the steps, you are not yet dancing but only learning to dance. A good shoe is a shoe you don't have to notice. Good reading becomes possible when you need not consciously think about eyes, or light, or print, or spelling. The perfect church service would be one we were almost unaware of; our attention would have been on God.

C.S. Lewis, Letters to Malcolm: Chiefly on Prayer

DO NOT MISS LEWIS' BEAUTIFUL DISCLOSURE from the early 60's: the aim of church worship services was to put God at the center of attention. Today, in too many of our 'worship' services across America, the question, *"How may we put God at the center of our attention?"* does not even reach the chalkboard of service planning meetings. We have usurped that position rightfully belonging to God – the center of attention.

I have attended many church-service planning sessions where questions of varied importance were asked. *How might we get more people to attend? What are people dealing with that we could address? Don't you think we should do more new/classic songs so that we don't lose the young/old that are now coming?*

It would be one thing if all of our shenanigans were actually aimed at focusing our minds on God. The resulting failure/s would be almost excusable. But the fact that too many church staffs are consumed with reducing everything to the lowest common denominator excludes what should be the only matter of consideration: How may we put God on display and push everyone's attention towards Him?

At a certain point we are not able to choose songs that everyone likes. But we are all able to tune our hearts to the declaration of God's wonder and greatness. At a certain point we are not able to choose a topic that is relevant to everyone. But the relevance of all scripture is timeless and universal.

How wonderful for Lewis that he was part of a believing generation (perhaps, historically the last) that focused their corporate togetherness on worship. Again, discussions on the matter of their successes or failures were only testimonies to their tactical aim! The correct answers to planning and participating in proper worship must begin with asking the proper question: How might we best make much of God?

Sixteen

THE TRUTH OF GOD AND THE TRUTH OF US

John 4:1-26

ALTHOUGH IT MAY HAVE BEEN ALONG THE MOST DIRECT ROUTE traveling from Judea to Galilee it may not have been the first choice of Jews to pass through Samaria. To the Jew it was uncouth and it was possibly unsafe. I personally believe that Jesus *had* to pass through Samaria (v.4) because He was *seeking* (v.23b); He had a woman and a nation to pursue as worshipers!

If we look closely at this encounter between Jesus and a Samaritan woman we find divine insight into the modern day discussion regarding seeker-sensitive worship services. It turns out that we are all engaged in a seeker-sensitive worship scenario. Only thing is, we are not the seekers – God is the seeker and we are the sought. It is God who pursues and we are the pursued.

And yet Jesus reveals that the human heart, in its fallen-ness, is seeking. Sadly, it seeks amiss. Jesus says, "[10]*If you knew the gift of God…*" She says, "[15]*Give me this…*" Jesus says, "*Go, call your husband and come here.*" It is within this dialogue we find the beautiful and humbling "truth" of it all (v.24).

At the beginning, Jesus reveals the truth of His divinity and His total efficacy in healing the human heart. And that is for us the most important truth because it is salvific truth! Of course, Christ seldom spells it out so literally and because of this, the woman misconstrues what He is really saying. So He confronts her with a truth that she cannot misunderstand – the truth of her sinfulness. It is what Christ is getting to when He tells her to go and call her husband.

It is only after Jesus reaches into her heart and exposes what only God could possibly know that she understands the first truth! And we should not have to imagine how she felt. This is the worship experience: The truth of God and the truth of us!

We hear the same words of Jesus that a woman in Samaria heard nearly 2,000 years ago, "*I am everything you need and all that your soul and heart has ever longed for. I am God and I satisfy. But in your wicked and idolatrous heart you try and fill your empty soul with husbands (or wives, or relationships, or drugs, money, work, houses, cars, pride, good deeds)."*

And against the backdrop of the shameful truth of these words we see Christ paint an incomprehensible portrait of love with the truth that He is seeking us!

Seventeen

DEFINING GOD IN WORSHIP

God is defined in the act of worship far more precisely than he is defined by any theology.

Roger Scruton, Contemporary British Writer and Philosopher

SOMEONE ONCE SAID THAT THE GREATEST CAUSE OF ATHEISM in the world today is Christians; who acknowledge Jesus with their lips and deny Him by their lives. Although this statement has some biblical plausibility (read John 13:35 and 17:23) it is not completely tenable (read Romans 1:18-31 and 2 Corinthians 4:3-4, et al.). Nevertheless, the sting of truth to the statement lies in its recognition of the disparity between what we (Christians) say we believe and how that belief is fleshed out!

Paraphrasing Scruton's quote Dr. Al Mohler writes, *"If you want to know what a people really believe about God, don't spend time reading their theologians, watch them worship. Listen to what they sing. Listen to what they say. Listen to how they pray. Then you will know what they believe about this God whom they worship."*

To be clear, this is not an issue of individual vs. corporate worship. The two cannot be compartmentalized. They are not mutually exclusive. They are, in fact, mutually dependent. Even more precisely, they are mutually enriching.

This being true, corporate worship may be the place that our best foot is put forward. In large part due to the fact that corporate worship is more often worship that is determined/focused (remembering that there is a difference between acts of worship and the act of worshiping).

If Sunday morning worship is, in one sense, putting our best (worship) foot forward, and it is also the primary way that God is defined to the world, then the manner in which we corporately worship should be a matter of great importance.

Even more important than what our worship communicates to the world is what our worship is communicating to the One whom we worship. We must define Him correctly if He is to be worshiped at all. If God is holy, and worthy, and deeply in love with His people, and longs for a deep and intimate relationship with us, and so on; our worship should with no confusion define these truths so that God "knows" that we know Him!

Eighteen

THE UNTHINKABLE REVERSAL IN WORSHIP

Then one of the seraphim flew to me with a burning coal in his hand, which he had taken from the altar with tongs.

Isaiah 6:6

THE ETYMOLOGY OF SERAPHIM COMES FROM THE WORD *SARAPH. Saraph* in all its forms is used to connote a burning fiery state. Rabbinic tradition taught that the name *Seraphim* clearly indicated their ceaseless and eternal revolution about the throne of God; and their "intense, perpetual, tireless activity…"

Revelation 4 takes care to describe these living creatures "full of eyes in front and behind" (v6) and in case we missed it – "full of eyes around and within" (v8). If there were ever any beings equipped to see the glory, beauty and holiness of God clearly, the seraphim were these. These beings have eyes all over them and even inside of them so that the penetrating, perfect presence of God is never without worshipful witness!

God creates with purpose. He is too efficient and intelligent for superfluousness. These four seraphim were created for worship only (…and day and night they do not cease…" v8b). They have wings, eyes and voices, each is a deep and rich testimony to the omniscience of their maker.

Steve Fry notes, these angels "are permanently caught in a transfiguration, utterly mesmerized by the One they worship. For time beyond time they have been worshiping God with no apparent care for their own existence, enraptured in the pull of divine fascination."

Any attention given to these marvelous creatures in scripture should only shepherd our gaze onto the indescribable One who made them.

So let us picture ourselves placed into the position we properly belong within the worship circle. We are Isaiah; supernaturally pulled into heaven's perpetual and only activity – worshiping God. And then something unimaginable happens: God turns His gaze on us! What love is this?

Do not think for a nano-second that Isaiah should have been so much as a blip on the radar screen of the seraphim. God's glory would have eclipsed any thing and everything. The creature was prompted!

Take some time to meditate on what happened in this context. Read between the lines of v6. You ought to notice God's love revealed in His seeing, sharing with, sanctifying, and sending (v8) us.

Nineteen

OUR GREATEST NEED AND JOY

The unspoken but increasingly common assumption of today's Christendom is that worship is primarily for us— to meet our needs. Such worship services are entertainment focused, and the worshipers are uncommitted spectators who are silently grading the performance. From this perspective preaching becomes a homiletics of consensus— preaching to felt needs— man's conscious agenda instead of God's.

Such preaching is always topical and never textual. Biblical information is minimized, and the sermons are short and full of stories. Anything and everything that is suspected of making the marginal attender uncomfortable is removed from the service, whether it be a registration card or a 'mere' creed. Taken to the nth degree, this philosophy instills a tragic self-centeredness. That is, everything is judged by how it affects man. This terribly corrupts one's theology.

R. Kent Hughes - Pastor and Contemporary Theologian

PERHAPS AN EVEN GREATER TRAGEDY IN CHRISTENDOM today exists in the irony that any blessing we may long for is found in blessing Him! This is not my way of glossing over the pain, sufferings and longings that exist in real ways. As if we only need to ignore our problems or pretend they do not exist and then they will suddenly go away.

People suffer unimaginable heartache in this world. Their pain is real and their problems are real and often very urgent. These realities cannot be denied and I am not suggesting other wise. I am only wanting God's perspective to be our perspective and it may begin with asking the *wrong* question: Does our most acute, desperate, urgent need ever become greater than God's glory? Our greatest need is God's glory!

Job's knee-jerk response to the news that all of his children had been simultaneously killed was worship! (read Job 1:13-22 and pay close attention to v. 20) Job's needs were not puny in that moment. In fact, his needs were so great that all he could do was worship. How far has the Christian idea of worship strayed from the biblical standard? I think it is a question we need to keep before us.

It is nothing for God to fulfill all our needs. It is not difficult for Him. It is difficult for us. I am praying for a paradigm shift in my mind and heart where my theology has been corrupted as it relates to the supremacy of God's glory. Worship must begin with God's glory not with our needs. For we do not lack certain things that only God can give, we lack all things and He is our All in All.

Twenty

GOD IS COMMUNITY

For where two or three have gathered together in My name, I am there in their midst.

Matthew 18:20

Let us hold fast the confession of our hope without wavering, for He who promised is faithful; and let us consider how to stimulate one another to love and good deeds, ***not forsaking our own assembling together****, as is the habit of some, but encouraging one another; and all the more as you see the day drawing near.*

Hebrew 10:23-25 (bold mine)

I CAN REMEMBER SITTING IN THE SECOND ROW from the front in my usual seat that I took for my "Trinity" class and hearing Dr. Kirkpatrick say the words "*God is community.*" I do not remember anything else about that particular lecture. I knew the phrase was important the moment I heard it. It has taken me some time to determine why.

To say, "*God is* ***a*** *community,*" I believe is not quite the same thing as saying, "*God is community.*" It may amount to the difference that exists between saying that "*God is loving*" and "*God is love.*" Both are true but one is a definitive statement on the very nature of God. It is more than a function or characteristic of God, it is a declaration on the make-up, essence and the very substance (ousia) of God.

The biblical truth that God is community (Father, Son and Holy Spirit) is a distinct problem for the person who says that they don't need to go to church to be a Christian or worship God. Or for the person who does not believe it is important to cultivate relationships within the context of a worshiping body of believers. So that they are able to attend Sunday morning services (perhaps at a mega church) listen to a sermon, sing some songs, and find their way home again, all without being noticed by any other person besides God.

While I would agree that this standard of Christianity is possible (and sadly quite pervasive), I would also say that simply because *it is* does not mean *it is good.* Anonymity and Christian worship are antagonists. Here is why.

We are never more like our God than when we are in loving community. And we may never reflect less the Glory of our God than when we are not. I think this is true of our relationships with our spouses, children, families, friends, etc. If all of this is true then, as it relates specifically to corporate worship, our highest praise is consummated within the context of our 'God-like' community.

Twenty–One

THE MIND OF WORSHIP

"What comes into our minds when we think about God is the most important thing about us.

A.W. Tozer

THE BEST QUOTES ARE THE ONES THAT SAY immeasurably more than the sum total of their words. This is one of those quotes. We likely cannot overstate the importance of our thoughts as they relate to who God is, what He is like, what He has done, what He is doing and what He will do. His intentions. His purposes. His character. Our destinies in this life and the next, hang in the balance of what comes into our minds when we think about God.

What we think about God determines our most elemental beliefs of our present reality and ourselves also. If God is omniscient what does that say of the human design? If God has unlimited power what does that say of our security? What does is it mean for us to believe that God has had His heart set on us before the foundations of the world? What does it mean for us to think that God is holy and perfect in totality?

Proverbs 23:7 says, *"For as he thinks within himself, so he is."* What comes into our minds when we think about God *indeed* is the most important thing about us! For what we believe to be true about God determines our eternal life (John 8:24) and our worldview (Romans 12:2). And what we believe to be true about God will also determine *whom* and *how* we worship.

Thinking deeper, erroneous thoughts about God will eventually determine *whom* we worship. Erroneous thoughts invariably lead to the worship of someone or something other than God. Legitimate, biblical thoughts only determine *how* we worship. For right thinking of God makes the matter of *whom* completely extraneous. Here's how:

If in our minds God is distant, detached, arbitrary, capricious or otherwise indifferent towards us, our lives will tragically reflect what our minds are convincing us of. A God like that is hardly worth our time, money, attentions, affections – our worship.

But a God who is intimate, loving, holy, just, righteous, and compassionate beyond any measure of understanding is uniquely and peerlessly worthy of our worship. Taking Tozer's lead then, might we say with some degree of certainty that *how* a person worships reveals what actually comes into their minds when they think about God?

What comes in to your mind when you think about God? Ask yourself how you worship – you'll find the answer there.

Twenty–Two

BECOMING WHAT WE WORSHIP

A person will worship something, have no doubt about that. We may think our tribute is paid in secret in the dark recesses of our hearts, but it will out. That which dominates our imaginations and our thoughts will determine our lives, and our character.

Ralph Waldo Emerson 1803-1882

Those who make them will be like them, and so will all who trust in them.

Psalm 115:8

ALL PEOPLE WORSHIP SOMETHING. Everyone worships and everyone worships all the time. Our lives revolve around ascribing worth and value to people and things. The very fabric of which we are made is woven with this desire to worship.

The bible says that we were created specifically and 'specially' (Psalm 139:14; Hebrews 2:7) to ascribe worth and value to the God who made us, giving Him glory above all else (read 1 Chronicles 29:10-13; Romans 11:36; Hebrews 2:10; 1 Peter 4:11; Revelation 4:11).

So what happens when we do not worship God? We replace Him with something else. It is inescapable. Our worship will be given and had. And built into this ineluctable worship system of being is the phenomenon that our worship will transform us into that which we glorify. (Any transformation, of course, relates to character not nature.)

Christ's revelation in John 4, that worship is foremost an activity of the spirit, is often misunderstood by those who want credit for worship but do not want to actually do any worshiping of God. People who think like this often say things like *"I worship God in my own way."* In worshiping God, however, there is no way in getting around exchanging our own way for God's ways.

True worship by nature resists dormancy especially as it relates to Jesus. True worship will not be anything if it is not eventually conspicuous! This is because worship is a non-stop activity of the heart. In other words, talk is cheap. Any one can claim to be a worshiper of God but as Emerson wrote *it will out.* We are only changed from glory to glory as we immerse ourselves in Him. Nothing else is able to transform us, only worship.

If you do not like whom you are becoming; in your thoughts, in your attitudes, in your behaviors then look to see who or what sits on the throne of your thoughts and affections. What is it that most consumes your imaginations? Your job? Finances? Spouse? Children? You? Our imitation of Jesus is refined in the crucible of valuing Him supremely.

Twenty–Three

DON'T COME UNDERDRESSED

Ascribe to the Lord the glory due His name; bring an offering, and come before Him; worship the Lord in holy array.

1 Chronicles 16:29

IT IS A RHETORICAL DEVICE TO SAY ANYTHING to the equivalent of "*Give God what He deserves,*" especially as it relates to His glorification. For what glory does not fundamentally and rightfully belong to God? Neither should it seem that this phrase is only a simple exhortation as if glorifying God is a personal preference or some kind of take it or leave it concept.

The Psalm we read in 1 Chronicles 16:29 is birthed within the context of God's nearness. It is the celebration of the ark (God's presence) coming to rest in the city of David. And it should be the instinctive response of God's people to thank Him for His presence. Therefore, as it concerns His people (and all of creation for that matter) giving God the glory He is due is an imperative!

About what God deserves or what is owed to Him, Asaph instructs us to begin with these: (1) an offering (2) your being/presence and (3) give holy attention to both. All three are equally important but even a cursory look at each one would take separate entries. I'll leave the first two for you to meditate on separately. Let us briefly look at the phrase "*worship the Lord in holy array.*"

Some translations have chosen something similar to "*in the splendor of His holiness.*" But my research has led me to believe that "*holy array*" is likely the best choice. It seems to fit better within the context of the imperative and the context of worship in the Old Testament. But what is meant by *holy array* and how does it apply to us today?

It seems the term applies literally to priestly dress, usually something breathable like linen but in any case pure and clean. It was a representation of the righteousness that would come through the perfect sacrifice of Christ. It is likely one of the clearest and most easily understood parallels bridging the O.T. and N.T., between the physical representation and the impending spiritual reality that would finally be realized in Jesus.

Indeed, even in the Old Testament dirty clothes was understood to be an illustration of our un-holiness as it was viewed under the burning light of God's gaze:

"Now Joshua was clothed with filthy garments and standing before the angel. He spoke and said to those who were standing before him, saying, 'Remove the filthy garments from him.' Again he said to him, 'See, I have taken your iniquity away from you and will clothe you with festal robes.'" Zechariah 3:3,4

"I delight greatly in the LORD; my soul rejoices in my God. For he has clothed me with garments of salvation and arrayed me in a robe of righteousness…" Isaiah 61:10

"And all our righteous deeds are like a filthy garment…" Isaiah 64:6

The bottom line is this: when we *"bring an offering and come before Him,"* we should come "dressed" appropriately. *"…for all of you who were baptized into Christ have clothed yourselves with Christ."* Galatians 3:27

I will confess my weakness of presumption on the goodness and grace of God in this particular area. That I often fail to properly confess my sin and ask for His forgiveness may not be lost in the freedom I experience as a worshiper.

I am not suggesting the erroneous notion that if, having received eternal life, you died before having a chance to recognize and confess every sin, your salvation may then be in peril. I am suggesting that there is something to the freedom we may experience in having our consciences cleansed on a regular, daily and even moment-by-moment basis.

"…let us draw near with a sincere heart in full assurance of faith, having our hearts sprinkled clean from an evil conscience…" Hebrews 10:22

"If we confess our sins, He is faithful and righteous to forgive us our sins and to cleanse us from all unrighteousness." 1 John 1:9

The great privilege we have in coming before the only and perfect God with a sacrifice, clothed with the righteousness of Christ must not be taken with the same deference as putting on a winter coat before going into the cold. The price paid for the privilege was inestimable!

Too many of us play in the filth of our sin and do not give a second thought to the condition of our spiritual dress as we enter in to worship. We wish to eat at His banqueting table without so much as washing our hands.

If we are able to relate to the embarrassment of being under-dressed for any occasion we have only a microscopic pinhole glimpse of what Asaph is trying to communicate when he says worship the Lord in *holy array*. Worship is the end-all black tie affair. Do not come under-dressed!

Twenty–Four

THE WEIGHT OF WORSHIP

Remember the perfections of that God whom you worship, that he is a Spirit, and therefore to be worshipped in spirit and truth; and that he is most great and terrible, and therefore to be worshipped with seriousness and reverence, and not to be dallied with, or served with toys or lifeless lip-service; and that he is most holy, pure, and jealous, and therefore to be purely worshipped; and that he is still present with you, and all things are naked and open to him with whom we have to do. The knowledge of God, and the remembrance of his all-seeing presence, are the most powerful means against hypocrisy.

Richard Baxter 1615-1691 English Puritan church leader

THERE NEARLY ALWAYS SEEMS TO BE what I can only describe as *weight* to the thoughts and writings of our fathers in the faith? When I read the old thinkers I often find myself saying things like, *"My God, how awesome You are!"*

Let us take for example the quote above from Richard Baxter. It is not the most beautifully crafted paragraph. It does not have the emotionally charged lyrical movement of a song or the imaginative and illustrative structure of a Milton or Donne poem (which also carry tremendous weight). The words he chose, in and of themselves, are not especially impressive or thought provoking and yet there remains within it an undeniable element of *weight*.

And within the sermons, songs, prayers and writings that permeate the theological landscape of our Christian heritage there lives this "lifting heaviness"! I am sure I would have loathed some aspects of how worship was fleshed-out back in much of our Christian history, granted. Nevertheless, I am also fully persuaded that I would relish the grandness of the overriding paradigm that sustained this *weight* within the worship community!

What paradigm is able to give birth and to nurture such a glorious weight? Our relative insignificance in light of God's transcendence! I could say it with a hundred different words but it boils down rather over-simplified to this – God is big, we are small. "Oh, Preston," you say, "Is this all you've got? You very nearly say this with every entry. You just mix the words up."

This is now entry #24 and I have come to the humbling and yet liberating conclusion that the answer to the question above is "Yes. This is all I've got." And though the entries seem to be getting harder to write I am certain that there is nothing more paramount to the heart of worship than this one central truth.

So, as long as He continues to impress this weight of truth upon my heart I will do my best to communicate it with the inebriating hope that what I say and write and do may bring more glory to God. The fact that it is becoming harder for me to find new ways to describe and magnify the difference between His heart and ours is really a testimony to that difference. I am finite, He is in-finite.

For the person who has not yet seen their exceeding sinfulness (cf. Romans 7:13) in the light of God's weight (glory, perfection), this entry, not to mention Baxter's quote and other literature similar to it, will likely seem a little over-the-top.

I mean, after all, God is loving and compassionate and forgiving is He not? Yes and yes and yes! But those things mean nothing apart from the context of a Holy, Righteous, Perfect, and Just God and His dealings with wicked, perverse and lawless people. What meaning has mercy outside the unimaginable wrath of God?

It is the holiness, absolute perfection, righteousness, justness, and the fact that God punishes sin, which informs us that God's love is immeasurable and inscrutable! God is awesome! May He lift us under the weight of His glory to this proclamation.

Twenty-Five

THE MIND OF WORSHIP II

They exchanged the truth of God for a lie, and worshiped and served created things rather than the Creator—who is forever praised. Amen.

Romans 1:25

Man, the only creature made in God's image, the only one who could think God's thoughts after Him, is the one who suppresses the revelation of God and gives glory to gross creatures rather than to Him. That is the chronicle of human history and is the most serious offense of all mankind and every individual - the refusal to honor God as God.

Dr. Joseph Pipa President, Presbyterian Theological Seminary

MOST PEOPLE WOULD EXCLUDE THEMSELVES from accusations of worshiping created things, especially as it relates to the ancient worship of animals, stars, moons, planets or people as gods (and other similar beliefs). Most rational people (believing in a creator or not) regard these kinds of beliefs as absurd, baseless, even foolish and rightfully so.

As the most intelligent creature in the animal kingdom of God we have come to believe that no other earthly creature is our equal or superior. In other words, they are not worthy of our worship. It seems, as a result, civilized societies have moved past nature worship and have moved toward something possibly even more offensive to God.

Thinking ourselves to be wise we suppress the glory of God evidenced in and by His creation and attribute it to a mathematically impossible number of random occurrences. In other words, we have substituted the once held belief that all of creation/nature has some intrinsic deep meaning (however often perverted in that belief) and exchanged it for the belief that creation is all the result of mindless and purposeless chance!

How offensive would it be to Michelangelo Buonarroti to hear the countless admirers of the Sistine Chapel praise the cathedrals resident cockroaches for its creation and beauty? Or how about the very figures that adorn the chapel's ceiling give praise unto themselves because "in all the world there is no other art quite so grand!"

Now imagine the throngs of visitors proposing that no one is responsible for the ceilings' beauty. It is nothing more than an illusion.

It's not actually a work of art at all. It is simply the natural colors, inclusions and shadows of the materials used in the construction of the chapel. It just happens to look like someone's been busy painting!

In reducing God's mind-blowing creation to such an unbelievable absurdity we offend Him on the deepest levels. Furthermore, the result of buying into this belief leaves humans atop all that has randomly occurred. And we live as if we are supreme. But the only logical conclusion in this belief system is to confess that we are the pinnacle of purposelessness!

(The great irony in this godless thinking is that we are no better or greater than the simplest form of bacteria. We are simply the result of a different set of random processes.)

And what about those who profess to be defenders of God's truth? We must carefully and continually examine our own understanding of God. Our worship is no worship (no different than the pantheist or atheist) if we are not worshiping in the whole truth of God's word.

Beliefs that conjure up ideas of 'the man upstairs' are not worthy of the one "who alone is immortal and who lives in unapproachable light, whom no one has seen or can see. To Him be honor and might forever. Amen." (1 Timothy 6:16)

Beliefs that conjure up ideas of 'God-Grandpa' are not worthy of the one who will hold all men accountable for every careless/idle word on the Day of Judgment. (Matthew 12:36)

Beliefs that conjure up ideas of an unreasonable and hostile God are not worthy of the one who "demonstrates His own love toward us, in that while we were yet sinners, Christ died for us." (Romans 5:8)

Beliefs that conjure up ideas of a God who wants to be our co-pilot or CEO are not worthy of the One who was beaten, whipped, sliced, pounded, gashed, gouged and murdered as penalty for our wickedness!

We are the only earthly creation designed in the image of God. We were purposed to worship intelligently! It is our only reasonable response. So let us purpose to worship God, not only with our entire heart, not only with all of our imagination but also with our entire mind!

Twenty–Six

Worship is Trusting

Abraham said to his young men, 'Stay here with the donkey, and I and the lad will go over there; and we will worship and return to you.

Genesis 22:5

If Jesus Christ be God and died for me, then no sacrifice can be too great for me to make for him.

C.T. Studd – 1860-1931 Missionary to China, India and Africa

REGULARLY WE SHOULD CONSIDER THE SACRIFICE ABRAHAM had determined to give to God. No greater manner of sacrifice could ever be imagined. It is not something we even want to think about for long. It is too difficult. Of course, God never intended to take Isaac in such a way (read Jeremiah 19:5).

Nevertheless, imagine the unforgettable lessons Isaac gained in seeing his father's obedience to God – lessons on the supremacy of God; the place and position of God in his father's heart; and the kindness, provision and timing of such an important God. It may be the most harmful belief of all for a child to perceive they are more important to their mother or father than is God. A horribly warped self-image results.

The application of the story for us, of course, lies largely in asking ourselves how far does our faith and trust in God extend. It should extend as far as God can be trusted, yes? To which we say there is no limit to the extent God can be trusted. He is limitlessly trustworthy. To which, all of His children say, "Amen!"

To which God usually says, "Put your money or your marriage, or your children, or your job, or your health, or your social status, where your mouth is!" Do any of us think there will be a time in this life when God will not be asking us to trust Him with something with which we think we can be trusted more?

God has shown me, relatively recently in my life, that when my worship becomes something I can do without sacrifice, without cost, without inconvenience, without effort, without concentration, without some apprehension, without preparation, and even on occasion without heartache, I have either come to completely trust Him with everything I am and have or I am not listening enough to hear Him say, "I want you to trust me with _______. "

A sacrifice of trust is an aspect of worship that needs my continual reflection and consideration. Thanks be to God for the sacrifice of His Son; through which we see that God is perfectly trustworthy.

Twenty–Seven

THE JOYFUL WORSHIPER

O come, let us sing for joy to the LORD,
Let us shout joyfully to the rock of our salvation.
Let us come before His presence with thanksgiving,
Let us shout joyfully to Him with psalms.
For the LORD is a great God
And a great King above all gods

Psalm 95:1-3

I have been to church today and I am not depressed!

Robert Louis Stevenson Novelist and Essayist, *journal entry*

May we be forgiven for looking the exact same as the agnostic that sits beside us! And singing as poorly as the unbeliever who came to find out what's going on!

Alistair Begg, Pastor of Parkside Church Cleveland

ARE WE (CHRISTIANS) TYPICALLY DEFINED BY OUR GLADNESS? When the word Christian enters the mind of a non-believer is it accompanied with an overall sense of joy? Is joy an indissoluble characteristic of your life? When you sing to the Lord (do you sing to the Lord?) is it voiced with gladness and joy?

Alistair Begg has noted that the Christian call to worship with joyfulness is not a call to superficial happiness. As if we are able to turn on and off our sincere emotions as easily as a faucet. Those who are able to do so are appropriately lauded as good actors. In any case, the call to joyfulness does not have much to do with emotions, although true joy should often find expression through them.

Joy is not an outward adornment. It is the inward ministry of the Holy Spirit (Galatians 5:22). If we often feel like we are on the outside of worship looking in, we must be honest with ourselves and ask the most important question there is as it relates to worship and everything else.

Are we in the faith? (2 Corinthians 13:5) A non-believer cannot worship God. The bible says that they are spiritually dead. If we have been made spiritually alive (saved) but still find our hearts indifferent to the worship of God then we fail to truly understand the person and work of Jesus.

The Christian's "unspeakable joy" (1 Peter 1:8) is hidden within the person and work of Jesus. Our joy is completely detached from current worldly, social and personal circumstances. It is conjoined to the One upon whom the full wrath of God was poured.

If our joy were in any way circumstantial then we would be some of the most offensive and insensitive people in the world or otherwise completely deceived and oblivious to the real sufferings that exist in our world and in our lives.

But the truth is that in Christ we have fullness of joy (Psalm 16:11): Not in our marriages, not in our children, not in our work, not in our countries or governments, not in our wealth – in Jesus!

I must say plainly that if our hearts are not "in" to worship it is because our hearts are not "in" to Jesus. We have inappropriately divided the affections of our hearts "in" to other people or things. And the result at the first sign of heartache is a corrupted joy!

The joy of the Lord is our strength because the strength of our Lord, the work of our Lord, the person who is our Lord is our joy!

Twenty-Eight

WORSHIP WITH MIGHT

You shall love the LORD your God ... with all your might.

Deuteronomy 6:5

And David was dancing before the LORD with all his might...

2 Samuel 6:14

Jesus answered ... "And you shall love the Lord your God ... with all your mind and with all your strength."

Mark 12:30

WHEN WAS THE LAST TIME YOU DID ANYTHING with all your might? And did it have anything to do with loving the Lord? It is more than interesting that Jesus chose two words to express *might* as the verses are translated in the NASB. For what does it mean to love the Lord with all our *might*?

Clearly, by worshiping the Lord with all our *might* it is not supposed that we should be in a perpetual state of exhaustion. Neither should we suppose that in any case it should be exclusively an activity in the physical. In fact, the first part of the *Shema* ("*with all your heart and with all your soul*") prevents us from being able to define it as such.

Nevertheless, we can be sure that our *might* (or our *mind and strength* as it were) is foremost a real and physical activity. Reasons of superfluity or hyperbole are not viable options for inclusion. Christ would not have clarified the text further if this were true.

So, when was the last time you offered every affection of your heart, every thought and attention of your mind, every intention and action of your will to the scrutiny and inspection of the holy glory of God?

When was the last time you abnegated the laziness of your flesh to kneel before your Creator in humble gratitude for granting you another peaceful night's sleep? Or when was the last time you refused the sinful advances of your flesh and instead turned to adore the One who paid the debt you could never afford?

Or do we show contempt for the kindness of God that leads us to repentance? So that we are able to live our lives with minimal thought and action toward that glorification of God to which Christ admonishes us. Do we let our minds wander through the teaching of God's Word? Or sing through clenched teeth songs about the supremacy of Jesus?

Let your hearts and minds be enraptured, engaged, enthralled, enthused by Him. When your concern for His glory renders you unconcerned about all other things you are loving Him with all your might!

Twenty–Nine

"DOING" AND WORSHIP

Martha, Martha, you are worried and bothered about so many things; but only one thing is necessary...

Luke 10:41-42a

In my life there have been times when I've become legalistic and tried to love God more by doing religious things. Yet ***doing*** *hasn't deepened my passion for Jesus. The only thing that deepens my passion is God-given revelation of who He is. (bold mine)*

Tim Hughes, worship leader/song writer

THERE ARE MANY CHRISTIANS WHO ARE RELIEVED to have included in scripture Christ's admonition to Martha. As if Jesus was supporting some notion that serving is an overrated function of religiosity and only those who are seated at the Lord's feet and listening to His word have any idea about what is important.

This kind of reading eventually leads believers into a "Dead Sea" Christianity – there are all sorts of spiritual minerals and nutrients carried in to the spiritual eco-system but the total lack of pouring out what is being poured in leaves the believer spiritually ineffective and lifeless.

Carried to its logical conclusion there is zero cultural and social relevance to the message of Christ! After all, we should only be concerning ourselves with bible study, singing songs of worship and praying. Everything else is trivial. Of course, any decent hermeneutic should prevent us from interpreting the interchange between Jesus and Martha in such a way. So what was Jesus saying?

Well, we know that serving others in the name of Christ is one of the central themes of the gospels. In fact, loving others as we love ourselves was the revolutionary teaching of Christ Himself. So, what Jesus was saying to Martha, I believe, had to do with Martha's desire to worship or serve Jesus by *doing.*

Human hands do not serve Jesus as if He needs anything, "as He Himself gives to all people life and breath and all things" (Acts 17:25). So it is important on one level to keep the physical Jesus within the context of the conversation.

"Martha," Jesus says, "you're busy *doing* for me; but *you* need *me*." At the heart of worship is the understanding that we need Jesus. And no amount of religious activity will ever change that.

So while some would like to use the words of Jesus to excuse their faith without works religion the issue has more to do with the way we see Jesus. For we know that any true worship experience begins with God's personal revelation.

We are misled if we believe that our religious works are helping Jesus or that they somehow have primary worth in the economy of God's kingdom. Nothing could be more important than getting a clearer look at God. For the more clearly we see God the more we are consumed with doing His will!

There is some level of irony in the fact that a true worshiper would never interpret the words of Jesus to mean that worship basically negates the need to *do*. Worship is the greatest motivator within the Christian heart to become doers of the word. If we want to be true servants of our King, it begins and ends at His feet!

Thirty

WORSHIP AND MISSIONS

Read John 4:1-38

Are you glad that Jesus Christ came into the world to repair all the injury that you and I have done to the reputation of the glory of God? Are you glad that Jesus came to do that? Or are you all wrapped up in 'I wanna get out of hell, that's all I want.' ...(are you) glad that the glory of God has been vindicated by the work of Christ! Does that make you say 'YES!!' inside? Or do you just want to go home and watch television?

John Piper – Contemporary Theologian/Preacher/Teacher

When it comes to discovering anything pertaining to acceptable worship the fourth chapter of John may be the most often referred to passage of scripture of all time. There is good reason for this. Nowhere else are we able to find the kind of categorically definitive statements on worship as we do here – words spoken out of the mouth of God Himself.

While preparing a sermon on the passage some weeks ago I noticed something intriguing about Christ's encounter with this person. It was something I had never noticed before. I had always thought of Christ's conversation with the Samaritan woman as nothing less and nothing more than a crucial teaching on the kind and quality of worship that is acceptable to God.

To be sure, the conversation is foundational to any good understanding of worship. It contains, by no stretch of the imagination, the single greatest quote on the quality of worship anywhere in the known universe – *"God is spirit, and those who worship Him must worship in spirit and truth (v24)."*

Certainly, we should be able to say that if any portion of scripture is specifically suited for the purposes of teaching us about worship it is this one. Indeed, I believe it has been an indispensable guide in directing Christians toward the heart of God since Jesus first spoke the words. But perhaps we have been missing an even greater point than the lesson on the quality of worship which is the principle of the priority of worship.

In the context, this divine meeting is foremost an evangelism encounter! Just look at the massive shift that takes place between verses

1-19, 20-24 and then 25-38. The quintessential 5-verse teaching on worship is couched within 33 verses of evangelism and other evangelism discourse. In fact, the woman seems to pull worship into the conversation out of nowhere. But there is a good reason for it. (We will talk about that a little in another entry.)

So, not only is the passage paramount in our understanding of the priority of worship, I might argue that John chapter 4 may be the most pivotal passage on evangelism in all of scripture as well! Here's why…

When Christ makes the statement that God is seeking worshipers within this evangelism context, He is making clear that the end of evangelism is the glory of God. Our salvation is not an end in itself – the worship of God is the end! To say that the end of the gospel is the redemption of humans is to demote God and position Him as the means or method in achieving that end. This puts man and his needs before God and His glory.

And while it is true that Christ IS the only means by which we must be saved I am simply refuting the idea that we are (our salvation is) the ends.

The person who has a hard time swallowing statements like, "God did not do it all for us," has simply misunderstood the end for which the gospel has been proclaimed to sinful man. God's glory and His creation's subsequent recognition and declaration of it will remain the eternal purpose! So if we say that God's glory is the end, and the means or method of accomplishing that end is the redemption of sinful man, we have read John 4 (on one level) correctly.

Why did I go through all of this? Primarily because we must be relentless in our belief and pursuit of the ultimate truth that God is supreme. If we do not guard our minds and hearts against subtleties like the one just discussed (that God is not the pinnacle of everything) we are prone to wander down the paths of man-centered idolatry.

May His greatness become your heart's consuming desire.

Thirty–One

GOD – WORSHIP'S PERSPECTIVE

Though He slay me, I will hope in Him. Nevertheless, I will argue my ways before Him.

Job 13:15

I have heard of You by the hearing of the ear; but now my eyes see You; Therefore I retract, and I repent in dust and ashes.

Job 42:5,6

JOB AND THE GOSPEL OF JOHN have always been my favorite books of the Bible. I feel like there is a similarity between the two. The similarity is in revelation. In one sense, every book of the Bible is like a window into God's heart. Some seem as small as pinholes; some seem obscured by the glare from the light of His glory; others are so high (Ezekiel, Daniel, Revelation) that even on the tips of my toes I can barely see above the sill; but the books of Job and John are like French doors for me!

Believing this, no complete discussion of worship could take place without giving the person of Job real thought. I touched on the astonishing knee-jerk reaction of worship displayed by Job after hearing that all of his children, 7 sons and 3 daughters, were simultaneously killed (Job 1:20).

I have often quoted Job 15:13 as my favorite scripture. Only the first part though, because I have nothing to argue only mercy to plead. But if there were anyone who could have made a case that an injustice had been perpetrated against them, Job would be that one (Job 1:1).

In my finite understanding of the situation I have to side with Job on this one. With the information given I would say Job did not deserve what happened to him. His friends disagreed. But it is more than just interesting that God never disagrees with Job.

God does not point out an egregious hidden sin, a pride filled spirit, some serious character flaw, or a lack of faith. That kind of response is reserved for humans. Sometimes we need to (or feel the need to) defend, explain or otherwise attempt to exonerate ourselves in light of questioning. But God is different. God never defends Himself – He reveals Himself.

We recently learned that a cherished friend in Hawaii has cancer. I hate cancer, partly because the word cancer does not actually define anything. Sure, we can assign it a location in the body (lung, brain, colon) but it is still ambiguous. And in so being, it is a coward. Like a murderer who has been found out but is still able to hide in darkness without really being caught. I can still remember the insidious effects that cancer had on my Grandfather.

I have another close friend who lives in Texas that is enduring unimaginable heartache in his personal life even as I write. For our friends, their wives, their children, there is most certainly the same feeling of unfairness in what they now must endure. My heart petitions for them in part (the part that is weak) along those lines. And God is big enough to be questioned. And if He is questioned with the heart of Job, a heart that says, *"Though He slay me, I will hope in Him,"* then I do not believe He is the least bit offended. It is the heart of a true worshiper.

I do not have the words for my friends. But Job calls out to them. In fact, Job calls out to all of us no matter where we are on our journey home. And the fact that his call was issued while still on the road of heartache justifies his cry. For that road makes sober realists of us all.

Again and again, the testimony of scripture to those wanting to be the worshipers that God seeks – get a good seat. God changes us, period. He is the ultimate reality; He is the right perspective.

Thirty–Two

AN INVITATION TO OUR GREATEST JOY AND GOOD

Those Divine demands which sound to our natural ears most like those of a despot and least like those of a lover, in fact marshal us where we should want to go if we knew what we wanted. He demands our worship, our obedience, our prostration. Do we suppose that they can do Him any good, or fear, like the chorus in Milton, that human irreverence can bring about 'His glory's diminution'? A man can no more diminish God's glory by refusing to worship Him than a lunatic can put out the sun by scribbling the word 'darkness' on the walls of his cell. But God wills our good, and our good is to love Him...and to love Him we must know Him: and if we know Him, we shall in fact fall on our faces. If we do not, that only shows that what we are trying to love is not yet God — though it may be the nearest approximation to God which our thought and fantasy can attain. Yet the call is not only to prostration and awe; it is to a reflection of the Divine life, a creaturely participation in the Divine attributes which is far beyond our present desires. We are bidden to 'put on Christ', to become like God. That is, whether we like it or not, God intends to give us what we need, not what we now think we want. Once more, we are embarrassed by the intolerable compliment, by too much love, not too little.

C.S. Lewis from The Problem of Pain

THE 'DIVINE DEMAND' TO WORSHIP GOD (and to worship Him alone) offends the soul of every man. It is the ultimate ignoble slap in the face because it challenges us at the point of man's first disobedience – prideful rebellion! We fight against Christ's worship, reduce it, remove it, ridicule it, scoff at it, rage against it, laugh at it, crucify it, and bury it, all that we might not have to submit ourselves to God's authority and do it! Why?

I had a recent encounter with a 4 year-old named Hunter. He was not happy about the car seat he was given because he wanted the one in which his younger sister Rylie sat.

Over the course of about five minutes I managed to reason Hunter down from his ledge of despair. And just as we were about to wrap things up something happened – a return to despair! The issue was not over comfort or fairness (it never is really) the issue was over being denied what *he* wanted. But what he wanted was not in his best interests.

The point of connection with the question of why we do not want to give God the glory that He is due is at the human condition of unreasonableness. We are (we must be) totally unreasoning. For it is only our good, which is His glory, that He calls us to His glorification. Are we so obtuse to reason that God's existence is enriched or diminished by our worship or lack of worship? If we do, we think too highly of our selves and too lowly of God.

God declares that He delights in us yes – amen and hallelujah! But be careful in believing that without our worship or adoration something of God is reduced! There is not a "human shaped hole in the heart of God that only we can fill!" He is from everlasting to everlasting, the beginning and the end.

God's worship is our good! It is our unreasonable pride that tells us anything different. So worship Him with all you have! Do it first because He deserves it. Do it secondly because it is our greatest joy and good!

Thirty–Three

ACCEPTABLE VS. UNACCEPTABLE WORSHIP

After coming into the house they saw the Child with Mary His mother; and they fell to the ground and worshiped Him. Then, opening their treasures, they presented to Him gifts of gold, frankincense, and myrrh.

Matthew 2:11

The gifts are intensifiers of desire for Christ himself in much the same way that fasting is. When you give a gift to Christ like this, it's a way of saying, "The joy that I pursue (verse 10!) is not the hope of getting rich with things from you. I have not come to you for your things, but for yourself. And this desire I now intensify and demonstrate by giving up things, in the hope of enjoying you more, not things. By giving to you what you do not need, and what I might enjoy, I am saying more earnestly and more authentically, 'You are my treasure, not these things.'" I think that's what it means to worship God with gifts of gold and frankincense and myrrh.

John Piper Contemporary Theologian/Pastor/Teacher

WE HAVE, IN ENTRIES PAST, LEARNED THAT OUR WORSHIP is our response chiefly to God's own revelation of who He is. Here in the second chapter of Matthew we should be able to see that the text is helping us along in our understanding of what a proper response to that revelation effectively looks like.

What is a proper response is often clarified along side of unacceptable responses. And as it was at the news that God was now with us, so it is some two thousand years past that there are essentially three responses to the One born Lord.

Firstly, there are those (many) who like the Scribes and Pharisees *initially* respond with indifference. In fact, Herod had to gather them and question them for information. We might imagine that the Jewish leaders of the nation might have been in the middle of a titillating and ongoing dialogue about a possible messiah.

After all, pagans from a foreign land had heard the news of a child born King and as a response launched a treacherous journey with meaningful and costly treasures with which to honor Him. But likely two years have passed since Christ's birth and the locals have not even raised an eyebrow? Indifferent.

Secondly, there are those who respond with outrage and pride. They are those that actively and willfully work to destroy and mock the name of Jesus. Every movement, idea, theory, philosophy and religion from the time of Christ's birth to this present day that have deliberately set themselves up against the person and work of Jesus are seed of Herod – that hateful rebellion. Evolution, atheism, religion, naturalism, materialism, and on and on and on are the offspring of Herod's hate.

I sometimes wonder which of these first two responses is more offensive to God. If an earthly King was besieged by hostile enemies it would be on some level a confession of His nobility. In the very least it would be recognition of His unwanted authority. But authority He admittedly possessed nonetheless!

But as it is with every human will and the worship of Christ, the indifferent will eventually acquiesce in humble repentance and faith or join the ranks of those who rage against the glory of Jesus! (It does not take long for the Scribes and Pharisees to pick up where Herod dies off.)

In fact, within the Kingdom of Heaven indifference is nothing less than treason. And in the end those who seem uninterested are exposed as natural enemies of God (Romans 5:10). Under the rule of Christ, there are only willing and adoring subjects or hostiles.

And so what of the third response? Joy and adoration! Have we the determined condition and purpose to see Jesus that has defined the magi for two millennia? Would we go to any lengths just to fall on our faces and proclaim His worth? What means are we willing to explore to proclaim and acknowledge His greatness and our smallness? Is Jesus the joy of our existence? Does He occupy the place of supreme worth and value in our hearts and minds?

Glory to God, all glory in the highest!
O come let us adore Him!
Christ the Lord!

This is the acceptable response.

Thirty–Four

LANGUAGES OF WORSHIP

[1]The heavens are telling of the glory of God;
And their expanse is declaring the work of His hands.
[2]Day to day pours forth speech,
And night to night reveals knowledge.
[3]There is no speech, nor are there words;
Their voice is not heard.
[4]Their line has gone out through all the earth,
And their utterances to the end of the world

Psalm 19:1-4

"I tell you, if these become silent, the stones will cry out!"

Luke 19:40

THE BIBLE SAYS that seas (roar), mountains (break forth into shouts of joy), trees (clap their hands), flowers (wrapped in greater splendor than fine clothes), the dawning and waning of the sun, even the furthest reaches of space to every star in every galaxy, have been brought into existence for one purpose: to "tell" of the greater glory of their Maker!

Even if we pretend that scripture is vague in defining the purposes of God in creating mankind, we would be near the height of arrogance to believe that as the supreme object of His creation we are somehow exempt from this supreme objective. Why would we be exempt? On the contrary, we have an even greater responsibility! It is we who have been given the inexpressible privilege of carrying the entire voice of creation on our tongues!

Notice that the third verse of Psalm 19 describes how the rest of creation is doing in fulfilling their created purpose. They are incredible communicators! They speak a universal dialect that every civilization from the beginning of time has been able to apprehend (Romans 1:20). It is to our shame the fact that we who have been made in the image of God, made as the image bearers of His infinite worth, are the only ones who have failed and continue to fail in the supreme objective of glorifying God.

Not only have we failed to express the truth of God's greatness we have misrepresented the truth of His nature and character. In a kind of cosmic dialogue creation is telling us the truth of it all and we are refuting it with lies.

Here's how we do it: When we lie, we tell the rest of creation that God is a liar. When we steal, we declare that God is a thief. When we hate, we testify that God is a murderer. When we worship anyone or anything other than God, we say that God is worth-less! And because of our failures the rest of creation groans in travail!

Our responsibility is to capture all of the "un-voiced" songs of the universe, all of the "un-uttered" truths regarding God's infinite worth and give life to them through our lips in the form of real, audible, discernable praise! *"Glory (Hosanna) in the Highest!"*

The words of Christ in Luke 19:40 should be coming in to clearer focus now. Rise up church with broken voices! Rise up all those redeemed of the Lord and say so!

Thanks be to God through Christ – He is our success!

Thirty–Five

THE INCREASE OF DECREASE

"He must increase, but I must decrease."

John 3:30

WITHIN THE HISTORY OF MANKIND JESUS SAID that there was no one greater than John, the Baptist (Luke 7:28). That is, John was the greatest person ever, excluding everyone ever born of the Spirit of God. The fact that the believer's "greatness" is not their own makes this truly an astonishing remark.

If we take the Holy Spirit out of the equation John stands alone as the pinnacle of human greatness! But we cannot miss the point of Christ's remark here in contrasting the goodness of man and the goodness of God. There is no comparison! The statement was not even intended as a tiny pat on the back for John. His disciples had already headed back to prison to see him before Jesus began teaching (Read Luke 7:18-28).

Nevertheless, the statement was made about the measured greatness of John. So then, what made John incomparably great relatively speaking? Well, there are many things that may have attributed to John's greatness but I believe his worshipful statement in John 3:30 reveals the crown of all his "excellencies."

Whatever joy John may have had in seeing thousands upon thousands upon thousands of his countrymen flock to hear and heed his testimony and receive a baptism of repentance ... whatever self-satisfaction he must have had in being immovably obedient ... or whatever gratefulness he may have had in being the one who was chosen as "the one crying in the wilderness..." were mere trinkets compared to the joy of magnifying the Messiah's greatness!

After all, he had a great ministry at one point. He started to turn a nation on its ear! And then it was gone. In what must have seemed like a moment he was taken from great recognition and great responsibility to a dungeon prison and an ignominious beheading on the whim of a girl's birthday wish.

Not that John didn't waiver just a bit . . . maybe? Initially, John was certain that Christ was the One! (Read John 1:34) He even says, *"I myself have SEEN…"* v.34. Not long after, while in prison, he sends two of his disciples to ask Jesus point blank, once and for all, *"Are You the Expected One, or do we LOOK for someone else?"*

It may be unfair to say that perhaps John's measure of decrease was more than he expected. But it would be nothing if not understandable would it not? From where John began to where he ended – and now Christ doesn't even have the time to visit him in prison with the answer to his noble longing!

There seem to be so many ways to go from here. But let us end on greatness. John's greatness, I believe, was measured according to his desire for magnifying God's greatness. He did not want the lead role because he could not handle the lead role! He wanted the role of an extra in a story where there can be only one Star and that role had already been filled in eternity. There are no auditions necessary for *Universe Idol.*

Be cautious of any teaching that places you in a starring role. Or any ideas that have as central to it, men and women in places of increase. All places of increase have been reserved, save the increase of decrease.

"For from Him and through Him and to Him are ALL things. To HIM be the glory forever! Amen (Romans 11:36)

Thirty–Six

THE SUPREMACY OF GOD'S GLORY

[29]...SO THAT no man may boast before God...

[31]...SO THAT, just as it is written, 'Let him who boasts, boast in the Lord.

Text - 1 Corinthians 1:18-31

YEARS AGO I USED TO WATCH SOME OF THE AWARD PROGRAMS on television, usually just the Academy Awards and The Grammy's. I have lost any taste for them now, mostly due to the fact that people do not know how to be praised. For me it is simply too painful and awkward to watch grown-ups being lauded. In some sense of irony the men and women most comfortable with their greatness were the ones most painful to watch.

In fact, I remember "The Academy" mercifully adding some sort of music prompt to stop the bleeding as it were. (I know it was implemented for the sake of time, but for me it was much more utilitarian.)

However, I did admire the ones that appeared to be genuinely uncomfortable with all the fuss; the ones that really wanted the spotlight turned on someone or somewhere else. But I liked best the very, very few of who were quick. That is, they basically said "Thank you," and graciously exited the stage.

The fact that we blow completely out of proportion the ability of people to make believe and sing (a gift or some random biological process – in either case a totally unearned ability) is not really the point of my illustration. The point has to do with the *pattern of this world.*

The wisdom of God is inter-fixed with His intentions of receiving all the glory! That is why *"The fear of the Lord is the beginning of wisdom, and knowledge of the Holy One is understanding"* (Proverbs 9:10). For who will boast in the face of something fearful? Only a fool. To begin to understand what makes the wisdom of God so wise we must have at the foundational level of our understanding this truth that God has geared all things to boast about Him.

In regard to the salvation of man God achieved His (and our) desired end in the only way and in a way the He only would receive all the praise! And yet He necessarily had to redeem us this way *"so that"* v29 and *"so that"* v31. The fall has made fools of us all. Our perverted want of adulation and exaltation rules over our divine need to glorify Him. And to understate the matter – God has helped us get over that hurdle by completely removing any human ability to boast!

Paul's admonition in Romans 12:1-2 is an admonition to the glorification of God to the death of human praise for the hope of ultimate joy. The boasting and glorification of man *is* the great *pattern of this world.* Thus divorcing ourselves from the world's pattern is our *spiritual act of worship.*

It is no surprise then that the world while working toward its unnatural and unholy end is simultaneously working against anything or anyone who would steal its glory. It is the reason the person of Jesus is reviled, ridiculed and hated by the world and all of its religions. Christ demands ALL the glory! (Apparently, no other god is nearly as obstinate as ours.)

Biblical Christianity contains the only teaching that shoulders all the blame on man and all the praise on God. The dividing line even among all cults and Protestant orthodox beliefs is the one that divides works and grace. We cannot help God even a little, and why? *So that* and *So that (1Corinthians 1:28 & 31).*

Thirty–Seven

GOD'S GLORY – OUR GREATEST JOY

My whole, more general, difficulty about the praise of God depended on my absurdly denying to us, as regards the supremely Valuable, what we delight to do, what indeed we can't help doing, about everything else we value. I think we delight to praise what we enjoy because the praise not merely expresses but completes the enjoyment; it is its appointed consummation.

C.S. Lewis, Reflections on the Psalms

Therefore, the reason God seeks our praise is not because He won't be complete until He gets it. He is seeking our praise because we won't be complete until we give it. This is not arrogance. This is love.

John Piper, Life As A Vapor

THE FALLEN HEART IS AMAZINGLY STUBBORN (or desperately wicked, Jeremiah 17:9). Within the human heart is pride enough to eschew our greatest joy and fulfillment for spite. *"Why does God get all the glory?" "What should make Him the object of all our affections?"*

What the host of biblical authors knew and what C.S. Lewis and many others have concluded is that God uniquely designed us to find our greatest joy in valuing Him. We can observe what Lewis did in finding that we not only praise what we enjoy the praise is the consummation of that joy. To bend the words from the theologically deep mind of Jerry Maguire "it completes us."

To withhold the praise that God deserves does not diminish God it diminishes us. If you desire more fulfillment, more joy, then you only desire to appreciate God more! The further we ignore our need for worshiping God; the further we invest our hearts in other people or things or ideas – the further away we are in finding The Joy of man's desiring.

And it is not as if God could have designed us any other way. He could not have, by definition, created something uncreated or more than Eternal. God is the most desirable and valuable thing in existence. It is only right that He points to Himself, as the One whom should be desired most.

It would not be humility that led God to direct us elsewhere to find our greatest joy. In knowing that we could never find what we are looking for outside of Him, God would then be cruel and sadistic and He would then cease to be God.

We should end our days regularly with something like this beautiful prayer from the book Life As A Vapor written by John Piper.

"Father . . . we have not seen and savored You as we ought. We have not worshiped You with the white-hot affections that You deserve. We have been lukewarm and half-hearted. Forgive us, O Lord, our merciful God. And lead us now into lasting joy. Enthrall us with Yourself. And break the power of lesser pleasures. In Jesus' name."

Thirty-Eight

THE APPRECIATION OF GOD

For My people have committed two evils:
They have forsaken Me,
The fountain of living waters,
To hew for themselves cisterns,
Broken cisterns
That can hold no water.

Jeremiah 2:13

BROKEN CISTERNS. WE ARE BROKEN CISTERNS. But how deeply gracious is our God! That we have forsaken the fountain of living waters and are so tragically debilitated that we are incapable of holding anything; yet He has lined our cracked lives with His own that He might fill us up!

I wrote last week *"If you desire more fulfillment, more joy, then you only desire to appreciate God more!"* (I trust no one took that to mean in any way that the desire is equal to the Desired.) I only intended to mean that we should want to see Him with rising admiration.

In other words, God should be appreciating in our hearts and minds. His worth and value should be increasing as it relates to our understanding and comprehension of His revelation of who He is and to the experience of His Spirit, power and love in our lives.

Lucifer's original sin was incubated in his heart's depreciation of God. It has since spawned every sin and evil. God levies the same charge against His people in the second chapter of Jeremiah. It is the same charge against us: God is infinitely appreciable in relation to the finite heart and mind but we find little or no satisfaction in Him. It is a crime to which there is no defense.

We should be praying to our good and His glory that He be our greatest desire! Our worship of God will rise in proportion to the increasing wonderment that we cultivate for Him. The beautiful equal and opposite reaction to His appreciation is the depreciation of every other competing worldly pleasure.

But this "God Inflation" is difficult work – just ask John the Baptist. And it is a great curse of the fall that we are by nature spiritual lotus-eaters, marked by indolence towards this grand desiring and so easily fatigued in the pursuit of it.

Everything to which we can find an end eventually depreciates in our spiritual economy. We were made that way on purpose. But be encouraged, we have not begun to plumb the depths of the riches of God's wisdom and dealings with His creation. He is infinitely fascinating to the desiring heart.

There is great hope for the Christian who wants to want God more. But we must get back to the fountain! We must abide there. God does not increase in our hearts while we nap in the tepid waters of our religious cisterns. We need to give the love, wrath, beauty, justice, goodness, patience, grace, mercy… of our God more thought.

Press on! He is unfailing.

Thirty–Nine

GOD'S INCREASING EXPECTATIONS

"Follow me!"

Matthew 9:9 (see also 4:19, 8:22)

"And he who does not take his cross and follow after Me is not worthy of Me."

Matthew 10:38

"Then Jesus said to His disciples, "If anyone wishes to come after Me, he must deny himself, and take up his cross and follow Me."

Matthew 16:24

"If you wish to be complete, go and sell your possessions and give to the poor, and you will have treasure in heaven; and come, follow Me."

Matthew 19:21

I SAW A BUMPER STICKER ON THE SECOND DAY OF THIS WEEK and it read, "Jesus said, follow me." I am not a fan of bumper sticker theology but this one I liked. In fact, I have not stopped trying to think about all that Jesus was saying with these two words since I read it on the back of an old Chevy van four days ago.

In today's culture the phrase could be understood by some to be little more than a call to pull little gems of wisdom and counsel from the life and times of Christ and apply these, as we find time, to areas of our life and relationships. But the call is a call to abandonment, the degree of which most of us would not agree to if we knew it at the start!

It begins with the least offensive invitation that of changing the direction of our lives to conform to the pattern of His Son's life. But the 'following' Jesus part is not as disagreeable as what 'follows'. Matthew gives us the literary equivalent to God's spiritual expectation of our increasing decrease.

Bonhoeffer wrote that when Christ calls a man "He bids him come and die." But according to Matthew it is not enough to simply "die." We must agree to die with nothing! If we do not think so, we simply have not read far (followed long) enough. By the time we (Christians) come to this realization (all of us eventually will, some sooner, others later) our greater realization is *"Lord, to whom shall we go? You have words of eternal life"* (John 6:68).

But this is nothing like a great bait and switch scheme, it is THE great exchange, a gift of grace. For the flesh profits nothing! We would never agree to exchange our names, jobs, possessions, families, friends and whatever else for gaining Jesus because we do not recognize the infinite worth of Jesus! Though we are beginning to.

This invitation of Christ literally means 'come behind me.' In other words, "All your hopes, dreams, desires, longings, all of you – come behind Me. I am the first and the last." There will be none before Him none beside Him.

I see clearer now than I did four days ago the truth of Christ's immeasurable greatness and the lengths to which He is calling each of us to follow Him. Consider for you what must now "come behind" Him.

God grant us eyes to see and ears to hear and wisdom to know the surpassing value of Jesus! For Your greater glory, for You are worthy.

Forty

WORSHIP - A MATTER OF SPIRITUAL GEOGRAPHY

15The woman said to Him, "Sir, give me this water, so I will not be thirsty nor come all the way here to draw."

16He said to her, "Go, call your husband and come here..."

19...The woman said to Him, "Sir, I perceive that You are a prophet.

20Our fathers worshiped in this mountain, and you people say that in Jerusalem is the place where men ought to worship.

John 4:15-26

IN THE FIELD OF LOGIC THERE IS A FALLACY termed *non-sequitur/sequitar. Non sequitar* literally means "does not follow." Usually, terms of fallacy are used in argument to keep the subject of debate on objective footing. But logical fallacies might also be observed in normal conversation as well.

Until very recently I always thought that the Samaritan woman's question about worship was somewhat of a *non sequitur.* It appeared to me that it was almost a way to simply change the subject. Like she very nearly plucked the thought out of thin air. But I am beginning to think differently. In fact, I think now she may have asked the only question that she could.

The realization that Jesus was "a prophet" (spokesman for God) is the turning point of the conversation for this woman. If you had the ear of God what truth would you want to know? For this woman there was nothing more urgent than the matter of worship – apparently.

Her question may have stemmed from the fact that Jesus just laid bare the shame of her life and spread it out on His lap before the two of them. Ponder the awkwardness for her. It is not a far stretch to imagine that she felt the need to 'get things right with God' as a result. In fact, I think there must have been at least an element of this Godly sorrow (which leads us to repentance Romans 2; Corinthians 7:10).

But for her the conviction is secondary to knowing the truth about where worship was acceptable to God. For if the place where she worshiped was erroneous then her worship was unacceptable. Conviction is rendered irrelevant within this context. She wants to know who is right, the Jews or the Samaritans. It was a gutsy question. Here is why I think so:

If the Samaritans were wrong and they could not hang on to the belief that they had the preferred place of worship then they were basically left with nothing! This was to the Samaritan the one thing that gave them legitimacy, as it were, at least in their own eyes. If the Jews had it wrong then the Samaritans would have reason to boast.

And then, as only and as He always does, Jesus flips everything right side up! The Jews and Samaritans were squabbling over the wrong location. The location of worship was a matter of spiritual geography (the heart) not physical geography.

Essentially, Jesus says, "You are valuing God misguidedly. God can only be valued in the heart! The basis of God's value is not measured by places and in times."

If God's worth is measured by us according to the church we attend, the money we give, the songs we like to sing, the version of the Bible we prefer, our denomination, we have not understood completely the conversation between Jesus and the Samaritan woman at the well.

These things and others do not measure God's value in our hearts they measure our value in our eyes. If our self-worth be increased for being right in what we believe about lesser things, or if God be diminished in our view for those smaller beliefs proved untrue, then we are still in conversation with Jesus at Jacob's well.

God, may You graciously remove the Mt Gerizims and Jerusalems in our hearts to make for Yourself more room to be worshiped and adored! Free us from the fear of being rejected for being wrong about insignificant matters. And free us from the petty pride that comes with being right about tiny matters. For Your greater glory.

Forty–One

WORSHIPING WITH CLEAR CONSCIENCES

... both gifts and sacrifices are offered which cannot make the worshiper perfect in conscience...But when Christ appeared...how much more will the blood of Christ, who through the eternal Spirit offered Himself without blemish to God, cleanse your conscience from dead works to serve the living God?

Hebrews 9:1-14

"But an hour is coming, and now is, when the true worshipers will worship the Father in spirit and truth; for such people the Father seeks to be His worshipers."

John 4:23

THE HUMAN CONSCIENCE IS AN OBJECTIVE GOD GIVEN witness to the truth of God's existence in righteousness and our spiritual lawlessness (Romans 1:19). It literally means, *with-knowledge*. But the conscience, like everything else, finds its greater purpose in God's glorification.

However, the old covenant with its emphasis on ceremonial, physical cleanness was powerless to cleanse our consciences and otherwise fit them for that greater intended purpose, in part, so that the immeasurable superiority of the work of God in Christ (the new covenant) could be seen more clearly at the "time of reformation" (Hebrews 9:10). The "time of reformation" being when Christ appeared.

Worship at its most foundational level was impossible prior to the sacrifice of Christ in large part because worship is foundationally experiential. I do not mean experiential in terms of subjective feelings (though I do not dismiss these out of hand) but in terms of spiritual togetherness with God. In other words, the sinful spirit of man and the perfectly holy Spirit of God were not simply inharmonious but utterly estranged.

Therefore, prior to the atoning work of Christ, "true" and "spiritual" worship was a non-option even for the believer in God. The spiritual option of worship was impossible for reasons mentioned heretofore (mutual spiritual hostility). And the "truth" option was not attainable for primarily the same reason. For no accurate appreciation of a person or objects worth can be estimated without genuine togetherness.

Could we truly appreciate the value of our children, our spouses, our friends, if we never lived in their presence? Oh, except for once a year when someone else could meet with them, on our behalf, but only to remind us how vastly separated we were?

In this case, humanity as a whole between the fall and the finished work of Christ on the cross was helpless to truly and fully (spiritually) worship the living God!

But thanks be to God in Christ! Can we seriously overestimate the words of Christ to the woman at the well whose conscience had just been gashed? And now those words have come to us!

There is no need to speculate on our freedom from guilt and shame! It is true for "*...Christ appeared...*" verse 11! Neither should we be confused over the purpose of Christ's perfect atonement. Verse 14 states that our consciences have been cleansed in order that we may serve (literally worship) the living God.

It is the same word used in verse 6 describing the performance of the priestly ceremonies as " the divine worship." But no longer are we in the outer-tabernacle! Christ, by His own perfect blood, has made a way for us into the very presence of God where before there was no way! And our hearts should leap in exultation at this truth!

So once again we find it is the Christian way that the glory of God be the end in all things. And we should love that it is this way! To be together with God with hearts and minds perfectly cleansed is to have no other desire than His magnification.

Forty–Two

HOLINESS AND LOVE, GRACE AND MERCY

Then Moses said to Aaron, "It is what the LORD spoke, saying,
'By those who come near Me I will be treated as holy ("sanctified" KJV*), And before all the people I will be honored (lit. glorified).*
So Aaron, therefore, kept silent."

Leviticus 10:1-7

EXODUS 24:1 INDICATES THAT GOD VIEWED Nadab and Abihu as men honorable for His service. They were two of only four men (along with Moses and their father Aaron) that were called by name to worship God along with seventy other elders as God confirmed His covenant with Israel.

The 8th and 9th chapters of Leviticus are entirely devoted to describing at length the consecration of these two young men and their father for priestly office. And then, upon their first actions as newly appointed priests, fire came out of the presence of the Lord and consumed them.

In matters of relevance there is little need to speculate what "strange fire" means. Moses' words to Aaron clarify the offense. Whatever was Nadab's and Abihu's "strange fire," it was not sufficient in declaring the absolute holiness of God to the praise of His glory.

I want to state clearly, if in 41 prior entries I have not, that nothing is more important to God than His own glory. God's statement, spoken by Moses to Aaron, is only one of many others that irrefutably support this truth.

What may not be immediately discernable in this case is that God, through the death of Nadab and Abihu, was being known as holy and therefore was being glorified. We should note that all failure to directly and properly declare God's holiness performs exactly this function in its subsequent judgment. Let us go a little further.

I believe the order of the entire universe, by God's intended design, is that everything that has gone out from Him must return to Him in praise. Hypothetically speaking, this would be the order of things even if it were not by intended design. For all things are formed with this immutable DNA.

Whatever has been, is, or will be made cannot do anything other than what it was or is intended to do. Therefore, God is not, as some suppose Him to be, a kind of tyrannical egomaniac eradicating anything and everyone who does not give Him what He wants.

In essence God is saying, *"I will be glorified. My way, which is good for you. Or your way."* It was C.S. Lewis who wrote that there would be two kinds of people on judgment day. The ones who say to God, *"Your will be done."* And the ones to whom God will say, *"Your will be done."* Not entirely theologically tenable, but I think we get the idea.

Getting back to the story . . . Aaron's two eldest sons have just been struck dead before his eyes and Moses says to him in essence, *"Because you are still in this worship scene* (vs. 7) *don't say a word* (vs. 3). *Don't even shed a tear or make a sound* (vs. 6a). *Or you may die!"* (vs.6b) Is that a mind-bender or what? Is God over-reacting?

At least a couple of things should be considered. Firstly, at the moment we begin to think that we have taken God's glory too far we have not. It only seems that way because our view of God's holiness is tiny and diminished.

Secondly, God has not changed. He is the same God. He has not mellowed or become less zealous for His name over the years as it were. His regard for His holiness is unchanging. The Hebrew word for "treated as holy" is the Greek word for sanctify or "hallow." (In fact, KJV's will note this in the Leviticus passage.) And so it is the first order of things as Jesus taught (all) of His disciples to pray, *"Your name be sanctified, treated as holy"* or *"Hallowed, be Your name!"*

I have a holy fear that even as I'm learning to appreciate the importance of God's glory more I continue to vastly underestimate its importance to God! In a sense the fear is invigorating. Like the fear we have of the ocean deep or infinite space. It is not an emotion of punitive origins because it is tempered with the belief that Christ's mercy triumphs over judgment!

Which brings me to my third and last and I think most important point. All the seriousness that God places on the glorification of Himself we can find at the cross. Christ our Savior absorbing the fist of God for us. As believer's we guard against cavalier, indifferent or otherwise "strange fire" attitudes not for fear of being consumed by the fire of God's judgment but for the love and grace and mercy of God to receive the judgment that we deserved.

May we weep for those who reject that payment and choose to pay the fine themselves.

Forty–Three

WORSHIP – OUR DELIGHT AND DUTY OF LOVE

He said, "It is finished!" And He bowed His head and gave up His spirit.

John 19:30

Now where there is forgiveness of these things, there in no longer any offering for sin.

Hebrews 10:18

NO RELIGIOUS ACT IN THE OLD TESTAMENT was complete unless accompanied with sacrifice; God designed the system with the intention of awakening a consciousness of sin and uncleanness. In fact, the system was utterly gory, repugnant, sticky and otherwise grotesque. (A foreshadowing of the death of Christ.)

Everyday, hundreds if not thousands of Jews would go to the temple to offer the appropriate sacrifices. Many of them were blood sacrifices. It is likely that there was a continual flow of blood that flowed from the temple – a constant, somber, putrid reminder of the high cost of sin.

Now hear the shocking words of John the Baptist – *"Behold the Lamb of God who takes away the sin of the world"* (John 1:29). The entire book of Hebrews teaches us that the blood of Christ was the sufficient blood offering for the sins of the whole world (cf. 1 John 2:2).

The single Greek word translated by the NASB as *"It is finished"* is *tetelestai.* It is an expression of completeness. In New Testament times many merchants would stamp *tetelestai* on notes that had been "paid in full."

The gospel truth is that we can offer nothing to atone for our sin. Jesus paid it all! It is the work of the enemy to convince unbelievers and believers alike that good works count toward our right standing with God. They do not. They count, yes, but not for righteousness, not for eternal life.

This understanding is essential as it relates to our worship of God because He judges the thoughts and intentions of our hearts. It is hugely important that the things we do and offer as worship are motivated only with the unalterable, singular devotion of glorifying God (read 1 Peter 2:12). They are otherwise considered bribes to a just and merciful God.

Any attempts to appease God's demand for justice tramples underfoot the perfect sacrifice of His Son and should be considered a serious offense to Him. Take some time to consider how the blade of God's justice was plunged into the Son as payment once for all.

Believing that we now have to make further sacrifice, or perform good works to ensure or assist in our salvation says to God that His unfathomable and inestimable sacrifice was not enough. May it never be! But let worship be the believers delight and duty of love.

Forty–Four

WORSHIP – PEACE BETWEEN GOD AND MAN

'Blessed is He who comes in the name of the Lord; Peace in heaven and glory in the highest!'

Luke 19:35-38

IN ANCIENT TIMES RULERS COULD DECLARE THEIR INTENTIONS by riding one of two animals. A warhorse would obviously communicate a position of authority if not outright aggression. It would have been the preferred status symbol. Nevertheless, in times when peace was the hope of nations, Kings would ride donkeys.

So we can see that Jesus was declaring His Kingship (nobility, royalty) as He mounted a donkey to enter Jerusalem. That is why the Pharisees were angry with Jesus and said to Him, *"Teacher, rebuke Your disciples."* But they were foolish and blinded. They could not see the kindness of God in and through the manner of Christ's humble entry.

We have not yet fully realized, any of us, mankind's God given fortune that Christ's first triumphal entry was a mission of peace! Thus Christ's words in verse 42, *"If you had known…the things which make for peace."* The cost for this peace would be immeasurable.

More clearly, Jesus was not bringing the peace or liberation that comes through conquering other nations and ruling over them (yet). His mission was infinitely greater than peace between earthly nations. He was bringing peace between God and man – *"Peace **in heaven**."*

And so it is the shout of every believer who has found peace with God through Christ, *"Blessed is the King from God who brings us peace with God, to Him be the highest glory!"*

For every Christian who mourns the rise of insurrection against our God of Peace and the belittlement of His name there is coming a day. For every faithful witness mocked, persecuted, tortured or killed for declaring the peace that God offers there is coming a day. For every blasphemer, idolater and fist shaker there is coming a day when Christ shall triumphantly re-enter.

But the donkey of peace will be conspicuously replaced and every eye (Revelation 1:7) will see Him coming on a white beast of war to judge the world in righteousness and to make war (Revelation 19:11).

May we who are called be faithful to proclaim that today is the day of salvation and there is still peace with God because of His forbearance. "*The Lord is not slow about His promise, as some count slowness, but is patient toward you, not wishing for any to perish but for all to come to repentance.*"(2 Peter 3:9) Pray for God's mercy.

Forty-Five

WORSHIP – OUR GLORIOUS PURPOSE

"Everyone who is called by My name, And whom ***I have created for My glory****, Whom I have formed, even whom I have made."*

Isaiah 43:7

"The people whom ***I formed for Myself****, Will declare My praise."*

Isaiah 43:20

"I, even I, am the one who wipes out your transgressions ***for My own sake****..."*

Isaiah 43:25

WHENEVER I WANT OR NEED A BEAUTIFUL REMINDER of the utter supremacy of God I read Isaiah chapters 43-46. No other portion of scripture so thoroughly and categorically declares the jaw-dropping uniqueness of our God, who is the only God. (For those who like to engage Mormons with sound doctrine there is no better place to make camp.)

Over and over again God Himself declares His exclusivity as the only one of His kind. These three chapters are the crucible in which all other claims to deity become dross. It is also the bedrock upon which our understanding of the Godhead exists. Combine Isaiah 43:10, 11, 12, 13; 44:6, 8, 24; 45:5, 6, 7, 14, 18, 21, 22, with Acts 5:3-4 (and others) with John 1:1 (and others) and you have a unique Being of One – in three persons.

We might imagine that a pericope so charged with God's claim to peculiarity is an extremely important passage of scripture. We would be correct. I encourage you to read the three chapters in their entirety. It is saturated with the voice of Someone who has too long been disregarded and misrepresented for lack of understanding. And now He is making it easy for everyone.

It is as if God were saying, *"Enough! I've put up with enough nonsense. Stop your chattering and hear this! I'm going to be unmistakably clear about who I Am and what the purpose is for all that I have done and made!"*

Perhaps more than most in our journey together so far, in discovering the supremacy of God's glory, these three chapters of Isaiah and the three verses cited above speak for themselves. Even if all we had were these three chapters for determining the supreme purpose of God, I would find it bewildering that so many called and saved are finding it so elusive!

We exist to glorify a purpose driven God! Let's get going!

Forty–Six

'JESUS IS LORD' – A CONFESSION OF GOD'S GLORY

...so that at the name of Jesus every knee will bow, of those who are in heaven and on earth and under the earth, and that every tongue confess that Jesus Christ is Lord, ***to the glory of God the Father****.*

Philippians 2:10-11

THE PURPOSE FOR WHICH EVERY LIVING THING (angels, humans, demons) will make the confession of Christ's Lordship is most often excluded from one of the most quoted passages in scripture. In so doing we are left (whether consciously or subconsciously) filling in the reason for ourselves.

In fact, the passage is often quoted as if to say that creation's greatest witness serves as a giant "I told you so" rather than a truthful declaration of God's peculiar mark of glory. If, as we have agreed, the glory of God is the end of all things, how would the confession that *Jesus is Lord* be the crowning mark of that glorification?

I mean, would not something more literarily special be better suited as a universal confession? With everyone speaking in their deepest voices saying, *"Long live Yahweh! There is none like Him. He is marvelous, wonderful, magnificent, beautiful, glorious, inscrutable, powerful, mighty, breathtaking, incomparable and inconquerable!"*

But no, with every knee bent in humility, will come the profound truth of God's greatest glory, which is His peculiar mark of glory, which is the humility of God – *Jesus is Lord.* Jesus is the glory of God! We only need to read verses 5-8 to see how:

*He existed as God but...

*emptied Himself to become a servant,

*not clinging to His radiant glory as God he took the humiliating form of a mere man

*humbled Himself to death

*further humbled Himself to a scandalous, ignominious crucifixion

It belongs to God alone the wisdom and ability to use the foolish things of the world to shame the wise and the weak things of the world to shame the things which are strong (1 Corinthians 1:27).

Creation's final confession is an overdue recognition of God's unimaginable humble greatness. *Jesus is Lord* is the whole of God's love and justice, His mercy and wrath, His kindness and holiness. *Jesus is Lord* leaves nothing left unsaid in confessing the glory of God.

Forty–Seven

HIS GLORY IS OUR GREATEST JOY

...if God does everything He does for His glory, does that make Him an egotist? Does the fact that He is bent on having all of Creation bow down and worship Him Make Him the world's biggest megalomaniac?

Louie Giglio, *i am not but i know I AM*

THE QUESTIONS ABOVE ARE BEST ANSWERED by the man who asked them, Louie Giglio. And I encourage you to read his book referenced above. But the questions are valid and certainly apply to the assertion of these writings regarding the supremacy of God's glory. So I thought it was only fair to give the line of thinking at least a cursory address. Just two thoughts here:

Firstly, there are only two categories or modes of existence: created and eternal. It would be insane to suppose that their intrinsic values are equal. Even within the created category of being there are differences in the worth of intentions, behaviors, skills, intelligence, etc., despite the best efforts of post-modern thinking (there is nothing objective; subjectivity is all there is). We do not, for example, teach our children that there is equal value in stealing and sharing.

Even if we were to take a post-modern line of thinking on the matter we could still say unequivocally that every people group in every civilization across time has valued some ideas and behaviors more than others, even if it is post-modernism!

With these beliefs then, we can begin to see why God is not a megalomaniac, He is simply being God (loving, wise, holy, perfect, and all of His "Omni's") in declaring His greater worth. For if God is infinitely more valuable than everything else combined, which He is, He cannot do anything but put Himself first!

It is not as if God is seeking to pump Himself up with self-adulation or gratuitous praise. Which leads us to our second thought that God's command for us to praise Him is nothing other than irrefutable evidence of His perfect, infinite love.

God is perfect, having no defect or need. Our praising Him does not in any way increase His greatness. It is ridiculous to believe that God's ego needs to be stroked and that is why He is commanding our worship. Rather, because of God's love He brought forth a uniquely created being (that's us) for the express purpose of, and with the mysterious ability to, enjoy His eternal perfectness.

In other words, He had nothing to gain, only perfect joy to give. In fact, to impart the ability for us to cherish and savor the things of God, He had to sacrifice His own Son. What a wonderfully selfless God!

Furthermore, as I have read both C.S. Lewis and John Piper express so wonderfully, our praise is also our greatest joy! It is our joy's appointed consummation. Our praise does not simply express our joy in seeing and savoring God's greatness it is the greatest part of our joy, it's the climax of our joy. God designed the system so that we might receive the unspeakable delight in praising Him! Unbelievable!

We are so depraved that we don't even know until the Holy Spirit reveals it to us, what is our greatest joy! Adultery, pornography, deception, ill-gotten gain and other indiscretions are no longer taboo because self-gratification is the new-god. Nearly everything is permissible under the shelter of "if it makes you happy." Indeed, our generation has reached a new low in calling good things evil and evil things good (Psalm 52:3; Isaiah 5:20).

And still God, in His grace, is calling all the nations, those who have eyes to see and ears to hear, to His praise! And in mercy He is patient with us, not wanting any to perish but all to come to a place of repentance (or turning toward the truth of God's infinite greatness) 2 Peter 3:9.

In conclusion then, to call us to any other purpose other than declaring His highest worth would be calling us to an endless and futile pursuit of real joy and fulfillment. So God is not a giant egotist but He is loving and kind and gracious when He calls us to His glorification.

Forty-Eight

SINGING TO GOD 'LOOKS GOOD ON YOU'

Next after theology I give to music the highest place and the greatest honor. I would not change what little I know of music for something great. Experience proves that next to the Word of God only music deserves to be extolled as the mistress and governess of the feelings of the human heart ... My heart bubbles up and overflows in response to music, which has so often refreshed me and delivered me from dire plagues.

Martin Luther, Here I Stand

Just as singing is a natural effect of joy in the heart so it has also a natural power of rendering the heart joyful . . . There is nothing that so clears a way for your prayers, nothing that so disperses dullness of heart, nothing that so purifies the soul from poor and little passions, nothing that so opens heaven, or carries your heart so near it, as these songs of praise.

They create a sense and delight in God, they awaken holy desires, they teach you how to ask, and they prevail with God to give. They kindle a holy flame, they turn your heart into an altar, your prayers into incense, and carry them as a sweet-smelling savor to the throne of grace.

William Law, A Serious Call To A Devout And Holy Life 1728

I THINK NOTHING SO EXEMPLIFIES CHILD-LIKENESS than does singing (and dancing). And not the kind of singing that now defines the music celebrity. That kind of singing almost exclusively glorifies the performer and is most often characterized by communicating sexuality, independence, bravado, violence and whatever else appeals to the flesh. I am talking about the kind of singing that gives no thought to self-awareness.

At the same time the kind of singing to which scripture exhorts us is not mindless. It does not engage in the pursuit of some kind of hypnotic numbness or other similar catatonic states. But worshipful singing does find itself dead to the scrutiny and inspection of anyone save God Himself. God glorifying singing finds its expression in wholly delighting in God and His greatness!

The scriptures are filled with exhortations to "sing to the Lord." The giant book of Psalms is itself a type of hymn/song book. (A Psalm is literally a song written with, and intended to be sung with, the accompaniment of instruments.)

In some manner of irony, our childlike singing is also a fierce weapon of war with which God allows us to conquer our/His enemies (cf Psalm 8). In fact, I believe much of God's emphasis on our singing out His praise has to do with spiritual warfare.

Satan and his horde cannot stand in the midst of God glorifying music and singing; that is, if God indeed inhabits the praises of His people.

For biblical support of singing as spiritual warfare I encourage you to read the Old Testament account of the invasion of Judah in 2 Chronicles chapter 20 (consider verses 21, 22 / spiritual as well as physical in this case) or the New Testament account of the imprisonment of Paul and Silas beginning in Acts 16:16.

Bottom line – singing is a matter of obedience. It is a God given imperative (I typed in *"sing to the Lord"* in Bible Gateway search and 60 scripture verses hit), and as we can see from the examples mentioned above, the imperative is not based on external circumstances or feelings. We sing because we ought! Furthermore, Psalm 147 says that it is not just ***good for us*** to sing to the Lord it is becoming. Nothing looks so good on us as does praising God!

So why do so many believers consider praising God with song a "take it or leave it" option of the faith? It is not! Beloved by God, blow the dust from your vocal chords and use them for their primary purpose! God could have just as easily created the human voice box with *only* the ability to speak. The ability to sing is irrefutable proof that God intends for us to sing (cf Luke 19:40).

It is pride that keeps us from singing His praise and it is injurious to us. Rather, choose to sing with a childlike heart – abandoned to the praise of His glory to the degree that King David's statement in 2 Samuel 6:22 becomes ours *"I will become even more undignified than this!"*

Forty-Nine

WORSHIP WORTH IMITATING – PART 1 OF 4

While He was in Bethany at the home of Simon the leper, and reclining at the table, there came a woman with an alabaster vial of very costly perfume of pure nard; and she broke the vial and poured it over His head.

Mark 14:3

IN A "MAN'S" WORLD the phrase "you ______ (run, throw, catch) like a girl" is a pejorative colloquialism. Sorry ladies, the fact is, you are inferior in matters that have no value in God's economy or eternity. Uh? Women are typically regarded as lesser in the world of reasoning too because they are more apt to ascribe worth to their emotions within the strict world of logic and fallacies.

Then this from the mouth of God, *"Truly, I say to you, wherever the gospel is preached in the whole world, what this woman has done will also be spoken of in memory of her"* (Mark 14:9). Only this morning has this phrase begun to strike me with the force that Christ intended it to have. Let us see if we can understand its magnitude a little better.

A unique and eternal God who lives in approachable light, whom no one has seen or can see, in whom is only perfection in every form, breathed His own life into a supreme creation (humans) meant to mirror His glory. But we willing moved from a secure place of perfect fellowship with God to objects of His wrath – a wrath that we are powerless to escape and when revealed will separate us from God in torment and spiritual death forever.

But God's love for us is so great that He sent forth His only unique Son to absorb the just wrath that we deserved. The torture and crucifixion of Christ who lived perfectly, never having sinned was the satisfactory payment for our crimes. And God raised Christ from the grave for it was impossible for death to keep its hold on Him (Acts 2:24)!

Because of these things and by no merit of our own, we now have the unthinkable right to be called children of God and live in perfect fellowship with Him again and forever. This gospel (good news) is granted to all who believe Him and all who receive Him.

Finally then, wherever this story, history's greatest story of God's unfathomable mercy and grace is told, the story of one of these sinful creatures (a woman) will also be told! If this is so, then we have to ask ourselves the question, "What did this woman do?" more seriously than we commonly do.

If God is willing, we will take a closer look at this woman in the next few weeks as we wrap up this journal journey (52 total). But to begin with, at least, on the most foundational level we can say this woman worshiped. And, of course, it should not surprise us now that the story of God should be accompanied with a story of worship, which is a declaration of His glory.

When we have finished, perhaps it will be one of the highest compliments for us to say, *"You worship like a (that) girl."*

Fifty

WORSHIP WORTH IMITATING – PART 2 OF 4

The anointing of Christ at Bethany.

Matthew 26:6-16; Mark 14:3-9; John 12:2-9

THE UNNAMED WOMAN IN THE ACCOUNTS of Matthew and Mark is identified as Mary, the sister of Martha, in the gospel account of John. It appears that Mary poured the expensive perfume on both the head (Matthew and Mark) and feet (John) of Christ then wiped His feet with her hair (John).

It may help in our discussion to remember that Mary is also the woman who was commended by Jesus for having 'chosen the better' as she sat at His feet (Luke 10:41-42). It helps, I believe, because all scriptural reference to this woman reveals that she possessed a singular devotion to the adoration of Christ that appears unrivaled in the New Testament!

We get the feeling that even when Jesus was not physically near, Mary was consumed with thoughts of Him. She simply knew Christ's importance and His uniqueness within the history of humanity. Nothing else explains her behavior in a spiritual light.

Last week we noted that worship was the over-arching spiritual point of the story. (The historical and prophetic aspect being Christ's preparation for burial.) Desiring to find the deeper fundamental principles relating to this general theme should lead us to ask ourselves why Mary's worship was so pleasing to God.

A closer examination of the contrast/s between Mary's *posture* and everyone else's posture, I believe, reveals the most crucial things. In #10 we actually began this discussion with the recognition that Mary came *prepared* to worship. Whatever it was that everyone else came to do that day it is obvious that it was not along the same lines of Mary's intention.

Not wanting to review #10 altogether but wanting to expand on this initial contrast we need to revisit some of the particulars of our story. The alabaster jar and its contents will suffice for our purposes here.

As there is general agreement among scholarship, I'll let J. Hampton Keathley III speak for everyone:

The "alabaster vial" refers to a cruise or flask made of white, semi-transparent stone which was used as a container for precious perfumes and ointments. It was full of "very costly perfume of pure nard." This was a highly perfumed ointment used for (1) cosmetic use for hot climates, (2) for anointing the dead for burial, (3) for ritual uses for anointing priests and kings, and (4) was considered a wonderful gift for a king because of its value.

"Nard," which defines the kind of ointment in the vial, was a plant found in the Himalayan Mountains. It was hard to get and very expensive … it was worth 300 denarii and the daily wage of the average working man was only one denarii. What she poured on the Lord Jesus was worth an entire year's wages!

With due deference to the thinking in #49 (emotional worship is to be sought) it would be erroneous to believe that what this woman did was either melodramatic or some kind of emotionally over-charged, rash act.

On the contrary! Because what Mary did was premeditated (#10) she would have had to overcome any number of "reasonable" thoughts or rationalizations or anxieties that would have kept her from her appointed task. Not the least of which was the value of the vial and nard. (Perhaps more on this next week.)

Furthermore, she would have decided before hand that her gift and expression of adoration was worth the risk of probable attacks and humiliation, both of which she did have to endure.

How many of us, or should I ask how many times have we thought to do something meaningful in the way of a letter, phone call, email, gift, etc., only to ignore the impulse long enough to have missed the opportunity?

That is not to say that every "good-inkling" that ever comes our way is to be followed. Rather, like Mary, we should measure the merits of the act and proceed if everything seems to favor the magnification of Christ even at the expense of our diminishment.

Loathing any trace of legalism I think it is only fair to investigate our physical postures as we worship both privately and corporately. Just for starters . . . have you ever had the "urge" to lift your hands as an expression of love, adoration, surrender, childlikeness toward heaven or clap your hands in applause for His greatness? How high and how loud?

Now in keeping with the posture of Mary . . . Have you ever *prepared* or predetermined to do these things prior to an encounter with God? As we noted in #10 this is how we ***enter*** His gates with thanksgiving. Is this 'girl' a tough act to follow or what? More next week.

Fifty – One

WORSHIP WORTH IMITATING – PART 3 OF 4

The anointing of Christ at Bethany.

Matthew 26:6-16; Mark 14:3-9; John 12:2-9

MARY CAME PREPARED. As I thought about our last entry I noticed that we stumbled upon an even earlier condition of Mary's posture, something that preceded her preparedness. Mary's prepared worship was conditioned upon her thoughts about Jesus. In other words, her beliefs about Christ constrained her to be prepared. And for what she believed to be true about Him she *loved* Him.

Do we *love* Jesus? This may be the most important question of all. Perhaps every important question relating to Jesus can be answered by responding "No" or "Yes" to this question. For no one can truly believe every claim of scripture as truth and yet be indifferent to the person and work of Jesus. Indeed, it would be utterly confounding to me why everyone is not in love with Christ were it not for the simple fact that some just do not believe.

Our worship, both privately and corporately, rises and falls on our view of God. A.W. Tozer put it best when he wrote, *"What comes into our minds when we think about God* [Jesus] *is the most important thing about us."* (For more on this quote refer to entry #21.) What came into the mind of Mary when she thought about Christ was the most important thing about her. For it cultivated this extreme expression of worship.

Is it not true that while we cannot dictate what was in Mary's mind when she thought about Christ, her thoughts were made manifest in what she did?

No modest Jewish woman in biblical times let her hair down in public. What Mary did was scandalous. Not only was the letting down of her hair scandalous, its offensiveness was magnified by the fact that her behavior was birthed by reasons of affection not need. Her indecorum was further compounded by the use of her hair (her glory cf. 1 Corinthians 11:15) as nothing more than a common dishrag.

Also, Alistar Begg has noted there were only two reasons why a woman in those days would possess such an expensive vial of perfume. Likely given to Mary in her younger **past** by her father as (1) a dowry

(present) or for her own **future** (2) burial. That sentence is a little messy I know, but it was the quickest way I could think of to illustrate what likely was expressed in Mary's worship.

She could have easily popped the top off the jar, poured a few generous driblets on Jesus, wiped His feet with her hair and then re-corked the bottle. But how much more was said by *breaking* the alabaster jar (so that it would serve no other purpose after serving its greatest purpose) and then pouring out her past, present and future with no reserve? Did she not *love* Him?

Those who do not love Christ can never be the kind of worshipers whom God is seeking for they cannot worship in spirit and truth. So how do we learn to love Jesus as He ought to be loved so that we may become the worshipers we ought to be? We worship.

That's right. We find an ever-increasing love for Jesus ***at His feet*** – the same way Mary did. It seems Mary was always at His feet (Luke 10:39, John 11:32; John 12:3). I do not have the time or space here to unpack this all the way, so I urge you to spend some time meditating on it.

But to give us a start, "at His feet" means essentially the same thing that we have been saying from the start, (2, 5, 6, 8, 11, 14, 16, 18, 21, 24, 29, 31) that we need continual and proper Divine sightings. These "views" of God feed our minds with the truth of God, which in turn incite our hearts with love for God. Our love for God is then fleshed out in worship. This is why we agree with Tozer that our worship rises and falls on what comes into our minds when we think about God.

It is not enough to listen to a sermon once a week that, sadly, may or may not help us get a better view of God, and then think little more of Him until next Sunday. Do whatever it takes to get at the feet of Jesus. Turn off the television, the ipod, the magazines, the books, the kids, the spouse, the oven, the housekeeping, and get at His feet. Just get at His feet.

Bottom line – If we want to worship God like Mary we have got to love Him like Mary. And to love Him like Mary we have to know Him like Mary. And to know Him like Mary we have to worship Him like Mary.

Fifty–Two

WORSHIP WORTH IMITATING – PART 4 OF 4

The anointing of Christ at Bethany.

Matthew 26:6-16; Mark 14:3-9; John 12:2-9

SO FAR WE HAVE SEEN THESE: (1) Mary loved Jesus. (2) Mary loved Jesus for what she believed to be true about Him, for what came into her mind when she thought about Him. (3) Mary's love for Jesus compelled her to physically demonstrate this love. (4) So she thought about how she could best show Him her love, what she thought about Him. (5) And she came up with (prepared) an extremely costly testimony. Without any words she said, "You're better than my life."

This is the extreme, radical posture of true worship. There is no other kind of worship really. And yet I believe that our worship becomes more extreme and more radical as we grow in the grace and knowledge of Christ. What I mean is that we began to see with ever increasing clarity that our "testimonies" are not near as extravagant as they should be in keeping with the measure of our knowledge of the greatness of God.

Perhaps two more bright elements should be mentioned (I am sure there are more) in the contrast between the posture of Mary and everyone else at the home of Simon the leper: decrease and increase.

Mary abjured whatever self-preserving or demonic influence that would have kept her grasping at the tiny bit of peer prestige or privilege for which we all desperately (albeit erroneously) long. Indeed, Mary excelled in the Johannine principle of worship (#35) that I call *the increase of decrease.*

Of all that I have learned in writing now 52 letters about worship and the supremacy of God's glory I value this most. In believing that this is one of the premier issues at stake in the glorification of God I would like to attempt to clear up what I mean when I say something like *my decrease for His increase.*

Those in whom we see the breathtaking principle best, people like John, Mary and Paul were not bent on depreciating themselves for the sake of finding some God-approved state of humiliation and lowliness. They were not anything like ascetics. As if their smallness was the target.

I think each of them had some ambition for becoming less important to themselves but this and everything else was driven by the greater part of the equation – His increase. That is why I would not say *His increase for my decrease* even though His increase is the first cause.

Anyone who has glimpsed the greatness of God naturally finds everything else worthless by comparison even our own worth. God's worth, His value, His glory, His greatness have no real competitors. We are torn between God and something else only because we have failed to see their true values. To have enjoyed God even for a moment is to have abhorred everything else in that moment.

Of course, when I use words like abhor I use them as measures of difference. We do not abhor our mothers, fathers, husbands, wives or children. Only we know God's worth is infinite, and if our attentions and affections for God are diminished by the attentions and affections for anyone or anything else we have gone wrong (cf. Luke 14:26).

Christ was supreme to Mary. Christ is supreme. May we see Him as supreme. May we love Him as supreme. May we worship Him, as He is – supreme.

www.ingramcontent.com/pod-product-compliance
Ingram Content Group UK Ltd.
Pitfield, Milton Keynes, MK11 3LW, UK
UKHW041935190726
13854UKWH00004B/1607